Natural
Intestinal Health

Third edition
10,000 copies sold

Updated September 2015

ISBN 978-0-9711155-4-5

Published by
Conrad LeBeau
10240 W National Ave #1896
West Allis, WI 53227
414-231-9817
lebeaubooks.com

i

Chapter 1
Restoring Intestinal Health

My personal experience with intestinal dysbiosis began in 1986. The previous five years had been very stressful for me as I was involved in helping farmers in the Midwest battle farm foreclosures with a novel range of legal challenges based on the "credit issue" that often only delayed the inevitable. By February of that year, I knew something was wrong, as a litany of health problems began to pile up. The list is quite long and included the following: food intolerances, indigestion, bloating, sore tongue, coated tongue, chest pains, fatigue, and insomnia with frequent nightmares. I also had colds and sinus infections, one after the other, and low body temperature. The digestion got so bad at one point I could not eat salads or raw food. When I ate a salad, what came out of the other end was still a salad – raw and undigested.

At that point I doubted that I could find a doctor to figure out the mess I was in, and I did not trust allopathic medicine and I had no health insurance. I decided, with God's help, to solve my health problems myself. I started by praying a lot and reading a lot of books on health with the kind of problems I was having.

It wasn't until 1991 when I felt good enough and had the courage to see a doctor for a complete exam. To my surprise, he declared me in perfect health. I thought to myself: "Wow! What he doesn't know." He doesn't know what I have been through, and besides, he is not entirely right, as "I am not in perfect health." I knew my health had substantially recovered, but I also knew I had some remaining food sensitivities and intolerances. I felt like a recovering warrior who had been wounded but survived a bruising two-year battle in a jungle. The time frame of my ordeal had begun early in 1986 and was over, except for an occasional relapse, by the end of the following year.

Are we missing something here? You bet. What did I do in the interim to recover? What did I do right and what did I do wrong? I am not going to share all the details of what happened in those two years as I could fill a thick book with that story, so I will cut to the chase and press the rewind button with selected excerpts.

In January 1986, I had read a book on the health hazards of mercury amalgams so I had them removed over a period of several weeks beginning in February of 1986. It helped a little and reduced my food intolerances, but most my health problems persisted, even with the amalgam fillings removed. At the same time I began using daily drops of food grade hydrogen peroxide (H_2O_2) with well water that was high in iron. While the oral H_2O_2 treatment got rid of my recurring sinus infections, it caused other problems that I was not aware of at the time.

The first is that H_2O_2 when taken with iron rich water reacted with the iron to produce free radicals. The free radicals did damage to my intestinal membranes, which caused me to develop a sore tummy syndrome. The other problem is that oral H_2O_2, like antibiotics, killed off my good intestinal flora, and that led to a yeast and Candida overgrowth problem. I learned later on that H_2O_2 can be absorbed by applying it to the skin. In this way the H_2O_2 could help cleanse the blood of pathogens and toxins, and would not kill off the friendly flora in my intestines; that is, of course, assuming that there were any friendly flora left. The lesson here is that while oral H_2O_2, like antibiotics, can save lives, you don't want to use either of these like daily vitamin pills or they will create other problems for you long term.

In May of 1986, I visited a local colon therapist and had my first colonic, and I noticed the first real and substantial improvement in my health. The colonic, that is the equivalent of about 25 enemas, had a dramatic and immediate effect on my well-being, digestion, and even my sleep. I looked ten years younger within 24 hours of having a single treatment. The colonic directly removed any fungal, parasites, and a pinworm infestation I had observed earlier after a bowel movement. I was so impressed with the benefits that I had a colonic every week for at least the next year.

The second thing that I did at the time that had a profound benefit on improving my health was drinking freshly made vegetables juices daily. I would juice apples or raw pineapple and combine this with carrots, celery, beets and parsley juice. A pint of juice daily seemed like the minimum I needed to feel good.

After I quit the daily use of oral hydrogen peroxide I made my third and greatest discovery – a smorgasbord of raw vegetables dipped in a mixture of plain yogurt and cold pressed flaxseed oil. I served this along with baked squash and green tea. Within 3 days, I noticed my stools returning to normal. It was like being reborn – the rest of my health problems seemed to vanish into the thin air.

The secret to this meal is the synergistic benefits of the anti-inflammatory effects of the omega 3 fatty acids in the flax oil combined with the non-fat yogurt. When I combined flaxseed oil with regular yogurt (with 2% or 4% milk fat) or with regular salad dressing, I did not get the same results or notice the same benefits. The only other oil I used with my salad was Cold Pressed Olive oil. I avoided using corn, canola, soybean, or other vegetable oils high in omega 6 fatty acid. Omega-6 fatty acids are pro-inflammatory and scientific research indicates they contribute to both heart disease and cancer. Cold pressed flaxseed oil is sold in health food stores and must be refrigerated. It also has a shelf life of about 6 months.

The most valuable healing meal I ever discovered. Call it the "Miracle Healing Salad"

The details of that most powerful anti-inflammatory healing meal are as follows:

Endive or (**Kale, Romaine lettuce,** and **Spinach**), **parsley,** sliced **yellow** or **green onions** with tops, **carrots, red or ripe bell peppers, one-half raw red beet - sliced, one clove of garlic sliced, hot peppers (may use canned jalapenos),** two or three **shiitake mushrooms, one Tbsp of raw sunflower seeds** (presoaked in water) and a couple of **ripe or green (Greek) olives.** You may add other vegetables like broccoli if you wish. Add **fresh lemon juice** over the salad and **cold pressed extra virgin olive oil.** Top with Paprika. Dip each vegetable in one cup of plain non-fat yogurt, with a tablespoon of **fresh flax oil** added. You may blend in dill weed, onion or garlic powder, and top it off with paprika. (Iceberg lettuce is not recommended – not enough nutritional value). Other raw vegetables, such as small amounts of ripe tomatoes or cucumbers, may be added to the salad, if desired.

With the salad, serve yourself 1/2 to 1 lb of baked or boiled **Squash**. Squash may be baked in an oven with added brown sugar, butter, and a few almonds. Pumpkin, squash, and sweet potatoes help to heal and rebuild the intestines. You may also eat whole **rye crackers** with your meal. You may add a little sea salt if desired to the salad. This meal should be eaten once a day. Foods in **bold** lettering are essential for this meal to perform its healing magic.

This meal has the God-given power to heal a wide range of chronic illnesses including most forms of cancer and heart disease. Its value is neither understood nor appreciated among health care professionals, or by the general population. It is beyond my power or anyone's power to take the healing essence of this salad and meal, bottle it, and place it on a store shelf for sale. That just won't ever happen. Example: Beta-carotene capsules won't replace the Squash. If you pit one part of this meal against the other, the foundation of this miracle meal will fall apart.

A variation to this meal for someone with missing teeth is to place all the ingredients in a blender and to puree it. Persons will need to eat each spoonful slowly and mix lots of saliva with it. If someone has such inflamed intestines that they cannot handle the raw pureed vegetables, then try mixing the yogurt and flax oil with cooked baby food or pureed cooked vegetables (like squash) and use this until the raw pureed vegetable blend can be tolerated.

You now have the main secrets of my recovery. The rest of my book is topping on this cake.

A ten point self evaluation guide

1. Appetite - Excellent, Good, Fair, Poor? Do you *eat because you feel hungry* or because *it is time to eat* or do you eat for pleasure when you are not hungry?

2. Diet - What do you eat? Wholesome grains, raw vegetables and fruits, cultured foods, easily digested proteins, freshly prepared vegetable or fruit juices - *or* - fast foods, pizza, white flour bread or pasta, French Fries, and other high temperature cooked foods?

3. How do you eat - Slowly and mix saliva with each mouthful - or - are you a fast eater and gulp your food down?

4. Digestion - How do you digest your food? No problem, good, fair, poor or I eat a meal and *it just sits there in my stomach* or does it come up and can you taste it hours later?

5. Output - Quality of Stools. Healthy stools are normally brown in color, large in diameter, and float on water – or –do you have unhealthy stools that are sinkers, and have a small diameter size indicating colon inflammation?

6. Urine - Color - a healthy medium yellow color (a sign of normal B vitamin presence and/or a breakdown of bile byproducts) – or - is it just clear - like a glass of water? Brown or orange urine may indicate hepatitis, liver, or other serious medical conditions.

7. Body Temperature - a normal 98.6°F - or - less. How much lower is it? Did you know that as body temperature drops below normal, so does the ability of your immune system to fight infections? Low body Temperature = loss of immune function.

8. Sweat – ability to – is essential to remove toxins from the cells. Inability to sweat may indicate a **selenium** deficiency.

9. Sleep - Great, good, fair, poor –or – do you wake up frequently and can't get back to sleep? Do you wake up feeling rested or tired?

10. Saliva pH - normal 6.4 - lower pH levels may indicate a calcium deficiency that impairs cellular and digestive function.

The answer to these ten points of health indicates balance or imbalance and gives you a personal overview of health-related areas that need attention.

Chemical preservatives kill friendly flora

Many chemical preservatives used to extend the shelf life of foods also suppress and stop the growth of friendly intestinal flora. They have long term damaging effects on intestinal health. Combined with refined carbohydrates, (that do not support the growth of good flora), manufacturers produce what I call plastic foods - unnatural in every way that set in motion a chain of events leading to all kinds of intestinal health problems including the two top killers - cancer and heart disease. Millions of people are on these disease-producing diets every day. The store shelves are loaded with these products - from breads to soda pop to lunchmeats. Chemical additives in processed foods, although approved by the FDA as GRAS (Generally Recognized As Safe), are not safe for long-term use when they prevent the growth in friendly flora (lactobacillus and bifido bacteria).

Common food preservatives include: **sodium benzoate** (a bacteria inhibitor), **potassium sorbate** or **sorbic acid** (mold inhibitor), **sodium nitrate** (carcinogenic), **sulphites** (may cause allergies), **propyl gallate** (cancer causing); **smoke flavoring** (cancer causing), and **artificial food colorings** (most types cause cancer). Salt (sodium chloride) is another food preservative and excessive amounts can also impair the growth of essential intestinal flora.

Note: Safe food preservative are **vinegar, citric acid, and vitamin C** Small quantities of **EDTA and BHT used** as anti-oxidants in food have no known adverse effects and are actually beneficial. However, "**reduced iron,**" added to enriched wheat and many commercial breads can produce free radicals and damage the intestinal mucus membranes, and should be strictly avoided. Reduced iron does not exist in nature - it is a highly reactive form of iron that can damage the intestinal membranes. The CDC reports of children dying from eating a handful of iron tablets.

The purpose of food preservatives is to increase the shelf live of food products. Food preservatives do this by suppressing the growth of both good and bad bacteria. Friendly flora are an essential part of a healthy intestinal tract and are absolutely essential for colon health. Without the byproducts of friendly flora fermentation in the intestines, mineral absorptions is impaired, and natural B vitamins and short chain fatty acid like butyrate are deficient or not produced at all.

The loss of butyrate alone deprives colonic cells of a basic fuel supply leading to a weakening of the membranes of the intestines – a condition that if not corrected will eventually lead to acid reflux syndrome, damage to the stomach lining, esophagus, small intestines and large intestines. Severe damage can lead to perforation of the intestinal wall requiring emergency surgery or even removal of the colon, and replacing it with an external plastic bag called a colostomy. Several forms of cancer are directly linked to consumption of chemical laden foods especially lunchmeats (ham, brats, hot dogs, etc). Most bread that sits on store shelves for several days at a time are usually loaded with all the wrong preservatives.

Another source of toxins that will damage the intestinal tract are chemicals from cigarette smoking. Smoking causes free radicals and ultimately damages all major body organs: from the liver to the kidneys, to the heart, to your eyesight, and weakens the immune system. Chemicals in cigarette smoke have been linked to an increase in acid reflux syndrome, a condition caused by toxins in bile (dumped by the liver) along with excess stomach acid production. Studies show that cigarette smoking when combined with drinking hard liquor increases the chance of esophageal and stomach cancer 100 fold.

Another source of toxic chemicals is liquid smoke. Liquid smoke is added as a flavoring to lunchmeat, fish, and other foods. Liquid smoke contains carcinogenic compounds that can cause cancer. Naturally smoked food is less toxic, providing it is done in the open air with plenty of oxygen (no cover over the food). This allows the aroma of the burning wood to be absorbed into the food with little or no smoke absorbed as a byproduct.

HEALTHY or UNHEALTHY STOOLS?

"large stools, small hospitals; small stools, large hospitals"
Author unknown

Healthy Stools:
Size - large diameter 1 to 1.5 inches
Color: medium/golden brown
Buoyancy - floats in toilet bowl.
Form: soft, formed round but firm
Little offensive odor.

Unhealthy Stools:
Size: Narrow - 1/4 to 1/2 inch wide (indicates colon inflammation - the more narrow, the more severe the inflammation)
Color: dark brown (indicates too much bile - diet is too high in fat).
Stools pale, gray, or yellow in color can indicate liver problems, either too little or too much bile.
Buoyancy: sinkers - will not float in water.
Form: mud like texture, hard lumps, mushy or diarrhea.
Offensive odor.

Do your stools float? Is your urine yellow?

No? This is a critical starting point to evaluate the primary cause of many gastrointestinal problems. If the stools are sinkers and your urine is clear, you may have a leaky gut and have a tendency towards some 17 other health conditions that are listed on the next page. *Stools float on water when friendly intestinal flora produce short chain fatty acids from fiber in the intestines and this causes them to be lighter in weight.* The sinkers indicate an absence of these short chain fatty acids and an absence of friendly flora. Yellow urine may be an indication of B vitamins presence suggesting active bifidus and bifido bacterium in the large intestines that produces these B vitamins; it could also indicate the presence of byproducts of bile secreted by the liver.

If you think you have healthy stools (floaters) and good intestinal flora, try this test. Stop taking all supplements with any B vitamins in them for 24 hours and check the color of your urine. If the color of your urine is clear, it means your large intestines do not have sufficient friendly bacteria (bifido-bacteria).

Exceptions on floaters: Sometimes stools will float when the diet is very high in fat. The high fat content of the stools may cause the stools to float giving you a false reading on the health of your colon. Try a low fat diet; if your stools sink, it means an absence of probiotics in the intestines and probably an overgrowth of Candida albicans. When stools float in persons on a high fiber, low fat diet, it usually means those good intestinal floras are producing short chain fatty acids that cause them to float in water. This is what you want - stools that float, are soft yet firm, have a large diameter and normal medium brown color plus urine that is not cloudy and has a medium yellow color and no strong odor. Note: Urine that is very dark yellow could indicate you are not drinking enough water. The first urine in the morning should be a deep yellow color.

17 health conditions linked to intestinal inflammation and Dysbiosis

1. Acid- Reflux Syndrome (heartburn)
2. Adrenal exhaustion
3. Blood stickiness (may cause fatigue and sensitivity to electrical fields).
4. Cancer.- colon, stomach and esophagus primarily.

5. Candidiasis and parasites.
6. Chronic Fatigue Immune Dysfunction Syndrome (CFIDS)
7. Colitis
8. Crohns disease
9. Diverticulitis
10. Fatigue
11. Food allergies and sensitivities
12. Heart Disease
13. Insomnia (calcium/trace minerals malabsorption)
14. Osteoporosis (calcium/trace minerals malabsorption)
15. Multiple Chemical Sensitivities (MCS)
16. Multiple infections of the GI tract (herpes, hepatitis, HIV, CMV etc
17. Ulcers

Case report: Her name is "Peg" and she told me she couldn't stand to be near microwave ovens or close to high electrical energy fields. She has multiple food allergies and candidiasis. She has been to many doctors. Some were sympathetic and others thought it was all in her head. After half an hour on the phone, I finally asked her about the characteristics of her stools. She was reluctant to talk about it at first. "That is a disgusting subject," she said. Finally she admitted her stools were the diameter of a pencil. I told her she had a toxic colon with severe inflammation. I suggested weekly Colonics plus daily enemas with a clove of ground-up raw garlic and vinegar added. (The clove of garlic and about 2 tablespoons of vinegar are added to a blender with a pint of water and processed at high speed for 30 seconds before placing it in the enema bag). I also suggested a high fiber diet, probiotics and a seawater concentrate. Her condition began to improve immediately.

It has been my observation and experience over the years that a combination of highly processed foods, overly cooked foods, chemical preservatives, many food additives, flavoring additives like MSG, foods allergies, food, spice, chemical sensitivities, excess salt use, occupational or emotional stress, and food colorings are the beginning of nearly all gastrointestinal health problems; some of which may take several years to develop. A smorgasbord of these highly processed foods can produce a cauldron in the stomach that can lead to heartburn, bloating, and indigestion. In extreme cases - including cancer - intestinal inflammation is so severe it leads to weight loss and malnutrition.

9

Inflammation caused by food and intolerance to food additives is at the root of most chronic intestinal disorders. Toxins produced by "unfriendly flora" (hyphaeated candida albicans, e-coli, gram negative bacteria, parasites and others) in the colon are also absorbed into the blood supply placing stress on the liver and kidneys for processing and eliminating the toxins. The liver has the task of breaking these poisons down into metabolites that are removed from the body through the bile, lymph system, kidneys and skin. Toxins in the large intestines contribute to liver toxicity, chronic fatigue, free radicals, poor blood circulation, blood cell stickiness, poor capillary circulation and an impaired immune response to viruses, fungus, microplasmas, bacteria and cancer. Poor appetite, impaired digestion and a toxic colon are common threads that link many of the chronic illnesses of our times.

Colonics and Enemas

The colon is a human sewer pipe that needs a good cleaning from time to time. For best results, have a professional colonic done weekly. Enemas: Blend one clove of raw garlic and 3 tablespoons of apple cider vinegar with a cup of water. Add mixture to a quart enema bag. (Hang enema bag, use a self-sticking plastic hook from and hang it about 15 inches above top of bathtub). The most convenient time to do an enema is after a bowel movement. Lie on back in tub in a knee to chest position. Allow mixture to flow into colon until it feels full. Enema solution need not be retained. Release and refill colon until enema bag is empty. Use bleach to clean the tub and shower when done.

Check your Yellow Page Phone Directory for **Colonic Irrigation** services. A good colonic removes waste matter that is toxic to the body. It gives you a fresh start. Colonics combined with the use of raw or cultured foods can help prevent many intestinal problems (colitis, crohns etc) and many more elsewhere in the body including atopic dermatitis, sinusitis, excess mucus in the sinuses and lungs, COPD, hypertension, heart disease, cancer, asthma, bronchitis, arthritis, and rheumatism.

Chapter 2
Natural Aids to Digestion

Slow eaters digest food better than fast eaters.

Digestion starts in the mouth with enzymes produced by the salivary glands. Hunger pangs in the stomach are the first sign that digestive juices are available. A watering mouth refers to the flow of saliva. Saliva production is stimulated by the scent of cooking food. While looking at appetizing food can be stimulating, the reaction of smell to food is usually stronger. While saliva is necessary to start the process of digestion, so is mastication – the chewing of food until it is broken down into fine particles and thoroughly mixed with saliva. This requires slow eating and a lot of chewing.

When food is thoroughly chewed (masticated), amylase in the saliva combines with the carbohydrates and starts converting the complex carbohydrates into simpler sugars. About 60% of carbohydrates are digested with amylase present in the saliva. Other enzymes are also found in saliva including lipozyme, protease, and lipase. Protease digests proteins and lipase digests fats. Some foods like *lemons and limes stimulate the flow of saliva* and will aid the process of digestion.

Persons who eat fast and gulp their foods lose the benefits of the first stage of the digestive process and cause a greater strain on the stomach, small intestines and pancreas as the food move along. If the food enters into the stomach only partially chewed, it may reduce assimilation of essential nutrients. It will also place stress on the white blood cells as they monitor the byproducts of digestion. Fast eaters are more likely to have an immune system under stress and less capable of dealing with other immune challenges like an infection. Fast eaters or persons who eat when they are not hungry will develop a wide range of gastrointestinal health problems over the long term including metabolic syndrome (obesity, high blood pressure, food sensitivities, allergies and many more).

Raw foods, fermented foods and food combining

For the most part, fermented foods like sauerkraut, kefir, and yogurt are more easily digested than non-fermented foods; however, whether you should primarily eat raw, fermented or cooked foods is best determined by listening to your own body. As the degree of digestive function and the condition on the stomach and intestines will vary from person to person, it is best to eat one food at a time to evaluate its effects on the digestive system. This is opposite of how most people eat who usually combine several foods at one meal. In nature and in the wild kingdom we do not observe animals combining several foods at the same time. Most birds and other wild animals will feed on just one food at a time, as this is how nature provides food. For example an apple tree does not also grow hamburgers, French fries and Colas at the same time along with the apples. Eating just one food at a time makes the process of digestion a whole lot easier. With a hamburger, you would do best to eat the hamburger meat first with a pickle or vegetables pickled in vinegar and follow this with a salad and the bun or preferably a slice of whole grain bread.

Of the three groups - proteins, fats and carbohydrates - proteins are by far the hardest to digest. When it comes to beef, raw beef is actually easier to digest than cooked beef as it contains natural enzymes. Actually, raw beef on rye bread with a slice of raw onion is actually a better choice than a cooked hamburger on a white bun.

Lunchmeats or smoked meats loaded with chemical preservatives and additives and fried meats are the worse possible choices. Meats that are boiled or simmered with water in a pan or cooked in a Crock Pot at a low temperature for several hours are far more easily digested than those cooked at high temperatures.

Foods naturally high in digestive enzymes

Raw pineapple is a good choice to eat with cooked meats as it contains a protein digestive enzyme called bromelain. Raw ginger root grated over meat or a salad also contains protease enzymes that digest proteins. Lemon juice or lime juice over meats and salads also helps with digestion. Apple cider vinegar and dill pickles also help with digestion of meats and especially in persons who are deficient in stomach acid. Sauerkraut with any cooked meal also helps due to the acids in the fermented cabbage. Red beets – raw - cooked or pickled help with digestion, especially meats, as beets contain betaine hydrochloride.

To summarize natural food digestive aids, these include-
1. Raw pineapple
2. Raw grated ginger root or aged candied ginger pieces
3. Lemon juice or slices
4. Lime juice or slices
5. Apple cider vinegar and other vinegars
6. Sauerkraut
7. Red beets

Take advantage of these natural foods to aid digestion before you spend a lot on money on pills. Avoid drinking distilled or reverse osmosis water that is acidic and mineral depleted. Drink only Spring, Artesian, Mineral or Well water. Avoid city tap water that has sodium fluoride or chlorine added.

Meats cooked at high temperatures stress the digestive system and promote cancer

Cured meats are especially cancer promoting, according to researchers at the University of Toulouse in France. (1) The researchers found that nitrates and oxidation "increased the number of preneoplastic lesions, which suggests colon carcinogenesis promotion" (1) in 344 rats used in the 100 day study.

In 2009, researchers at the Vanderbilt Univ in Nashville, TN report that *"High intake of meat, particularly red and processed meat, has been associated with an increased risk of a number of common cancers such as breast, colorectal, and prostate"* Zheng and Lee state that Heterocyclic amines (HCAs) are a group of cancer promoting amines found in cooked meats and particularly in well-done meats and are some of the most potent mutagens detected. They report on the results of a 10-year study that has found a significant increased of cancer from well done meats.

1. Meat processing and colon carcinogenesis: cooked, nitrite-treated and oxidized high-heme meat promote mucin-depleted foci in rats. Santarelli RL et al; Cancer Prev Res (Phila). 2010 Jul;3(7):852-64. Epub 2010 Jun 8
(2) **Well-done meat intake, heterocyclic amine exposure, and cancer risk.** Zheng W, Lee SA. *Nutr Cancer.* 2009;61(4):437-46.

13

Why eat grass-fed beef? Omega 6 fats are linked to breast cancer - Monsanto's GM corn with Roundup increased cancer 200% in lab rats

A study in Sweden in 2008 found that a diet high in omega 6 polyunsaturated fatty acids (PUFAs) (from corn) was associated with an increased risk of breast cancer. Sonestedt E et al state: *"a significant increased risk was observed among those with high intakes of omega-6 PUFAs."* A substantial number of studies have found a link between high intakes of omega 6 fatty acids and an increased risk of cancer. On the other hand, omega 3 fatty acids found in flax seed oil and in wild fish have had protective effects against many types of cancer. Like wild caught fish, grass-fed beef is naturally high in Omega 3 and very low in Omega 6 fatty acids. Grass-fed beef is clearly a safe choice while corn-fed beef is not.

With grass-fed beef, another problem is avoided – the eating of Monsanto's genetically modified (GM) corn with the bt pesticide in it as well as exposure to Monsanto's herbicide "Roundup." A recent study from France found a 200% increase in cancer as well as liver and kidney failure in Wistar rats fed Monsanto's bt corn over a two year period. (2)

(1) Int J Cancer. 2008 Oct 1;123(7):1637-43.
(2) Food and Chenical Toxicology Sept 11, 2012.

Cayenne, Horseradish and Gentian as metabolic stimulants for digestion

Cayenne (Red Pepper) is one of the most underrated spices in the plant kingdom. Cayenne increases the flow of blood in the capillaries, veins and arteries, as well as increasing body heat and metabolism. *Cayenne combined with a little apple cider vinegar will put a growl in your stomach.*

Cayenne also stimulates the hunger response when taken before meals. Try taking one cayenne capsule with 1 teaspoon of apple cider vinegar in a glass of water before meals, then gradually increase the dose. Do this each time before you eat and soon you will find strong hunger sensations returning. If you need to do more to get your appetite back, add ginger root or horseradish if necessary - add horseradish to coleslaw or use it on boiled cabbage and carrots.

Both cayenne and horseradish stimulate digestion, metabolism, and circulation throughout the body. Both help fight water retention and tumors. Cayenne will help lower high blood pressure and increase it in persons who have low blood pressure. Cayenne helps heal ulcers by stimulating the growth of new mucus membranes.

Tabasco sauce can be sprinkled on poached eggs or over cooked vegetables. It is best to use a low sodium vegetable juice as salt is usually added to these cayenne sauces.

Horseradish: For beginners, go easy especially if you have a sensitive stomach. Horseradish can be mixed with coleslaw dressing or used on beef brisket and added to cooked cabbage, brussels sprouts, cooked carrots and rutabagas. Horseradish can be placed on crackers topped with cheese or sliced raw vegetables. Horseradish is great for lung and sinus infections.

Other herbs: Gentian root is used in "Bitters" sold in liquor stores and can be mixed with vegetable juice. Health food stores also sell herbal bitters. Oregon grape root - 20 drops twice daily is also beneficial.

Breakfast or Dinner cocktail - to 6 ounces of low sodium tomato or vegetable (V8) juice) add 1/2 tsp. of Tabasco sauce and/or 1/4 teaspoon of herbal "Bitters" with Gentian. Squeeze some lemon juice into this and bravo, you have a real zesty cocktail that will increase your metabolism and immune function.

Chapter 3
The Colon and the pH factor

pH represents the "potential Hydrogen" absorbing capacity of a substance. A pH of "0" means a substance is as acidic (i.e. sulfuric acid) as it can get and will absorb no more hydrogen atoms. At a pH of 13, a substance can absorb lots of hydrogen ions (i.e. ammonia is alkaline). The digestive process requires hydrochloric acid in the stomach but needs a neutral or slightly alkaline pH in the small intestines. When the food reaches the large intestines, the pH drops to around 6 in healthy individuals.

A lower colonic pH should not be confused with saliva pH where the normal resting value (between meals) should be 6.4. When the saliva pH is either too alkaline (above 6.4) or acidic (below 6.4), it adversely affects digestion and enzyme function.

Friendly acid-producing bacteria help to move colonic pH (down) in an acidic direction. When the pH of the colon is alkaline (above 7.0), all kinds of unwanted pathogens from viruses to fungus to bacteria set up housekeeping and can cause havoc with your immune system by producing toxins and harmful chemicals that burdens the liver, kidneys, and the immune system.

HIGH COLON pH LINKED TO CANCER, CFIDS and CANDIDIASIS

Bech K et al (18) found that in measuring the pH of the feces that *"Significantly higher pH values ..... were found in patients with cancer than in normal individuals."* He wrote, *"These results support performance of intervention trials with lowering the pH of the colon with the object of cancer prophylaxis...."*

Research published in the Journal of AIDS, PNAS and Nature's Medicine have found that up to 86% of all HIV virus lives in the intestines. If the pH of the colon is higher than 6.0, cell-free HIV can infect CD4 cells and continue replicating, but when the pH is less than 6.0, cell-free HIV permanently loses its ability to infect new cells (20).

Anecdotal reports from persons with CFIDS, cancer, and/or candidiasis who have had stool samples analyzed report the following:

1. High pH values usually in the 7.0 to 9.0 range.
2. Little or no acidophilus found in the stools.
3. Low butyrate levels indicating low bifido bacteria counts.
4. High levels of candida albicans and other unfriendly flora.

These abnormal values are most often associated with food allergies, leaky gut syndrome, and a weak intestinal wall. Frequently, persons with CFIDS, candidiasis, and severe food allergies often find that the only foods they can tolerate are vegetables and proteins. Persons with CFIDS, candidiasis, hepatitis, and cancer that are doing poorly always report stools that sink (in the toilet bowl) and sometimes have a small diameter indicating inflammation in the intestines.

Leaky Gut Syndrome contributes to food allergies

The role of the immune system in the gut area is not well understood. The immune system becomes more involved in the intestines as the health and integrity of the mucus membranes of the gastrointestinal tract deteriorates and a condition known as "leaky gut syndrome" develops.

The membranes of the gut acts like a fine filter to allow in usable byproducts of digestion and to keep out the larger ones that cannot be used by the body. The more "leaky" the gut, the more undigested proteins pass through the intestinal membranes and the more involved will be the white blood cells of the immune system to stop these unwanted byproducts of digestion from entering the blood supply.

White blood cells, the foot soldiers of our immune system, attack all foreign substances in the body (viruses, bacteria, fungus as well as unusable byproducts of digestion). Unwanted protein byproducts of digestion are foreign proteins called "antigens" that leak through the gut. This sensitizes the immune system to these byproducts of digestion causing mast cells in the intestines to secrete histamine. Histamine is a potent stimulator of acid production in the stomach. Milk, eggs, chocolate, shellfish, and wheat gluten are common food allergens (3).

Leaky gut syndrome → histamine → IL-6 → chronic immune dysfunction

"Mast" cells that are located in the intestines produce histamine. When the mast cells are sensitized to a certain food, they will release histamine on contact. In response to stress on the immune system from unusable byproducts of digestion, histamine is not the only chemical produced, Immunoglobulin type E (IgE) and interleukin 6 (IL-6) levels also increase (4,5,6). Both types of histamine (H1 and H2) induce increased production of IL-6 and other proinflammatory cytokines in the mucus membranes. IL-6 is elevated in persons with chronic insomnia, AIDS, CFIDS, candidiasis and cancer. (8).

LGS substantially weakens an effective immune response against all illnesses associated with chronic immune dysfunction including candidiasis and cancer.

What causes Leaky Gut Syndrome (LGS)? Answer: junk foods, sugar and corn syrup

Excess consumption of sugar and corn syrup is a major cause of intestinal dysbiosis leading to leaky gut syndrome. Sugar feeds the growth of parasites and yeast as well as weakens the immune response. A diet high in sugar combined with a diet low in insoluble and soluble fiber causes a lack of bifidus and other bifido-bacteria in the colon. This leads to a shortage of short chain fatty acids like butyrate that are fuel to build a strong intestinal lining. Butyrate deficiency contributes to leaky gut syndrome. Other factors include infections of the gut mucosa including candidiasis, parasites, worms, and certain viruses.

Lab Test for Leaky Gut and Malabsorption.

A test for both leaky gut syndrome and malabsorption is available from Great Smoky Diagnostics Labs, 63 Aillicoa St, Asheville, NC 28801 800-522-4762. Another test is to check for a type of white blood cell called "eosinophils." Researchers have found eosinophil protein X (EPX) activated in fecal samples in all types of inflammatory bowel diseases - including Crohns disease, ulcerative colitis, food allergy, and other conditions (7).

Chapter 4
Bifido-bacteria and butyrate are essential for colon health

Butyrate is one of several short chain fatty acids produced by certain friendly intestinal flora known as bifidobacteria (Bifidus, B. Longum and others). Besides butyric acid, bifido-bacteria in the large intestines also produce other short chain fatty acids including lactic acid, acetic acid, proprionic acid, and even formic acid. Collectively, these acids suppress the growth of most viruses and pathogenic bacteria that inhabit the large intestines. In other words, the good intestinal flora suppress the bad and the reverse is true - unfriendly flora will suppress the good intestinal flora, until and unless you make dietary choices that tilt the balance of the intestinal environment in favor of the friendly flora.

Researchers have also found that in the small intestines, bile from the liver that contains toxins will kill off the acidophilus. Scientists in the Netherlands have found in experiments on rats that the supplement calcium phosphate can neutralize the toxins in the bile resulting in an increase in acidophilus levels and a decrease in salmonella (21). Besides altering the bile contents to no longer be hostile to the acidophilus, researchers also found that calcium phosphate reduces the amount of bile produced.

Butyrate deficiency is a major cause of leaky gut syndrome and other Gut issues

My interest in butyrate was awakened in 1999 when a lady with CFIDS reported taking the daily supplement, Butyrate, and noticed an immediate improvement in her gastrointestinal symptoms. A second person who has had CFIDS for 10 years and has developed severe Acid-reflux syndrome along with multiple food allergies reported significant benefit from the use of a butyrate supplement. In a toxic colon, stool analysis for butyrate finds that it is consistently low.

Restoration of a healthy gastrointestinal tract requires action on two fronts. 1) destroying infections like candidiasis and parasites that damage the mucus membranes and 2.) providing nutrients from a diet and supplements to rebuild the mucus membranes. Butyrate is one of the most important fuels for stimulating the growth of new mucus membranes in the intestines. Wheat bran, oat bran fiber, and foods high in inulin or FructoOligoSaccharides (FOS) have been found to strongly increase bifido-bacteria and butyrate levels.

The growth of bifido-bacteria is nourished by indigestible carbohydrates including - FructoOligoSaccharides (FOS) and inulin, naturally occurring carbohydrates found in high fiber foods but especially in artichokes, chicory, onions, garlic, asparagus and bananas. A bowl of French onion soup or a large baked onion contains about 2 grams of FOS.

Butyrate is fuel for colonic cells. Butyrate stimulates the growth of mucin (a component of mucus) and the mucus membranes of the intestines. The mucus membranes are our first line of defense against infections getting into our body. A thick layer of mucin (in intestinal mucus) prevents colonization of candida albicans and other pathogens. As the mucus is sloughed off, so are the pathogens.

A long-term absence of bifido-bacteria in the large intestines causes a severe butyrate deficiency that ultimately leads to leaky gut syndrome, inflammation, and a weakening of the intestinal wall. When the wall weakens sufficiently, the colon can collapse, or a rupture of the intestines can occur requiring emergency surgery. Less serious but important conditions like Diverticulitis, colitis, ulcers, and food allergies can develop from long-term butyrate deficiency.

Butyrate deficiency can also predispose or lead to colon cancer. A wise person will pay at least as much attention to the colon as to their teeth, hair and fingernails. A toxic colon is the result of a lifetime of eating refined carbohydrates, foods cooked in fats and cooked at high temperatures while avoiding foods that are high in fiber (whole grains, vegetables). The best foods that support the growth of bifidobacteria are onions, asparagus, garlic, artichokes, chicory, buckwheat, bran, glucomannan and under-ripe bananas. Foods that support the growth of lactobacillus strains are winter squash, pumpkin, buckwheat, bran, carrots, raw garlic, and raw dark green vegetables - endive, kale, parsley, and romaine lettuce.

Inulin or FOS from whole food sources strongly promotes the bifidus and to a lesser extent acidophilus while whole foods high in calcium promote acidophilus. Biotin will also promotes probiotic growth and keeps Candida albicans in a single cell and non-invasive state.

Other substances that support the rebuilding of the mucus membranes are: vitamin A, cabbage juice (raw or cultured), buttermilk, Gamma Linoleic acid, horsetail herb, L-Glutamine, slippery elm and witch hazel tea. L-Glutamine works much better when biotin is taken at the same time. Butter and buttermilk contain small amounts of butyrate but alone are not sufficient to meet your needs for butyrate.

Eden Foods, manufacturers of "Bifa-15" a microencapsulated source of B Longum, report that as many as 400 different kinds of bacteria may inhabit the gastrointestinal tract. When the colon becomes the primary feeding ground of unfriendly flora like e-coli and candida, a condition called toxic colon develops and the pH of the colon becomes alkaline. Ammonia, amines, and other toxins produced by unfriendly flora, impair liver function and immune function.

As a general rule, most of the unfriendly flora like a pH that is alkaline while the friendly flora like an acidic colon. A predominance of friendly flora creates an environment that suppresses the bad bacteria. The reverse is also true - if most of the flora in your gut are unfriendly, they will create an environment hostile to the friendly flora. This is indeed a war of microbes and we are in the middle of it. The food choices we make daily determine which side prevails - the good flora that keep out the bad or the healthy bacteria that promotes illness. Having a predominance of friendly flora in the colon is not an option for a healthy intestines, normal digestion and a strong immune system - IT IS A REQUIREMENT!

Scientific research on Butyrate

Scientists have found that butyrate increases the production of mucin, a component of mucus, which provides a protective barrier throughout the entire gastrointestinal tract (9). In experiments on rats, researchers found that glucuronic acid, a component of a variety of fibers, significantly increased mucin production, as did sodium alginate, acetate and butyrate. Acetate, like butyrate, is a byproduct of bifido-bacteria fermentation of carbohydrates in the colon.

In animal experiments, scientists have found that butyrate hastens the repair of damage to the mucosal membranes of the colon induced by heat or detergents (10). Scientists have found that butyrate helps prevent colon cancer and induces Glutathione S-transferase to detoxify carcinogens (11). Wheat bran was found to significantly increase butyrate levels (12).

In January, Cheryl C., who has CFIDS, told me she took 1 butyrate capsule with meals 3 times a day and noticed an immediate improvement in her gastrointestinal symptoms. Over the counter butyrate is available through Ecological Formulas or Allergy Research. It comes in the form of calcium butyrate and magnesium butyrate, which is a buffered form of butyric acid. Usually 1 or 2 tablets or capsules with each meal produces noticeable results in a few days.

Once you have a healthy colon and normal healthy stools (floaters) you will not need to take butyrate as a daily supplement. However, when your colon is toxic, butyrate supplementation would be well advised.

Supplements: There are many good supplements that help to implant intestinal flora when used along with a diet naturally high in fiber (whole grains, fruits and vegetables). Some of the most important strains are: L Acidophilus, L Rhamnosus (for the immune system), B. Bifidus B Longum and to help reduce food sensitivities - L Plantarum, a probiotic that improves immunity against cancer. All these strains increase the levels of SCFA's or short chain fatty acids that are so essential to intestinal health.

Bifa-15 - contains B Longum (distributed by Eden Foods) Bifa 15 is microencapsulated and can be found in some health food stores. B-Longum promotes intestinal IGA that helps with defense against intestinal pathogens.

Ojibwa Probiotics Powder contains 6 major probiotics (L. Acidophilus, L. Rhamnosus, B. Bifidus, B Longum, L Salivarius and L Plantarum). It is available as a powder and is sold in health food stores (Ojibwa Tea of Life, Denver CO).

Butyrate capsules reduce food intolerances

Calcium and magnesium butyrate are available in tablet or capsule form in health food stores. Persons who take 2 capsules with each meal 3 times a day report a substantial reduction of food intolerances and sensitivities in 5 to 7 days. After 30 days of use and the restoration of normal stools, try stopping the use of the butyrate capsules and see if the food intolerances return.

There are two manufacturers: They are Ecological Formulas Concord CA 415- 827-2636 and Stephen Levine Ph.D, of Nutricology, Alameda, CA 510-487-8526.

Vitamin D from Sunlight and intestinal health

An article on vitamin D deficiency by Maegules s. et al published in J Dig Dis. 2015 Aug 27. reports that while vitamin D deficiency is a worldwide problem, that

"the prevalence of vitamin D deficiency in patients with intestinal malabsorption syndromes, including cystic fibrosis (CF), celiac disease (CD), short bowel syndrome, and inflammatory bowel disease (IBD), is higher than that in the general population, indicating the presence of disease-specific causative factors."

In this article, the authors report that insufficient exposure to sunlight and the inflammation that results from a deficiency of vitamin D is a causative factor in the development of intestinal malabsorption syndrome. Since the immune system resides primarily in the intestines, the development of food sensitivities and allergies are likely linked to blood levels of vitamin D.

With 63000 published studies on vitamin D, a deficiency is widely reported to exist in 75% of the general population but especially in persons with intestinal problems and immune suppression. Deficiencies of vitamin D are now linked in published studies to over 50 disease conditions.

The Life Extension Fdn reports that a vitamin D blood level of 50 ng.ml is a good target range. The reference range is from 30 to 100 ng/ml. I took 10,000 i.u. of vitamin D daily for 6 weeks to achieve that target range. See your doctor for more information.

Chapter 5
Scientific Research on the Benefits of Probiotics – our Friendly Flora

Bacteria are everywhere from the air we breathe to the water we drink to the food we eat. They are on your clothes and skin. Most bacteria are good and beneficial for our health. Bacteria are microbial scavengers - they eat what is not alive. They recycle the basic building blocks of life to be used again to feed the creation of new life.

Think of a world without bacteria. Nothing would decompose. We would have the dead carcasses of dinosaurs here from 50 million years ago. Dead trees and plant would not decompose without bacteria. The oceans would be filled with dead fish. Without bacteria, the whole world would have died a long time ago. In fact, without bacteria to recycle what dies, it would not even be possible for human beings to exist on planet earth today.

Good bacteria are on our skin, in our mouth and in our intestines, and are essential for a normal functioning immune system. Antibiotic soaps destroy friendly flora on our skin and make us more vulnerable to harmful bacteria. Our skin is the largest organ we have for eliminating waste and toxic byproducts of cellular metabolism.

Activated white blood cells of our immune system reside in the lymph nodes of our intestines. Specific types of white blood cells like macrophages monitor the byproducts of digestion and seek to block foreign proteins from entering the blood supply. The health of the intestines (mouth to colon) is the foundation for a balanced immune system for the prevention of disease.

Health stresses occur when undigested proteins or partially digested proteins are absorbed into the blood supply – when a condition known as leaky gut syndrome exists. This causes inflammatory immune reactions that create food sensitivities and food allergies to develop. Having an abundance of friendly flora in the gut creates an inner garden that crowds out the weeds – the unfriendly flora including yeast overgrowth, molds, parasites, etc that cause adverse health effects.

Natural wild strains of intestinal flora come from many sources including raw mother's milk, kefir, yogurt, yogurt cheese, sauerkraut, and cultured vegetables. Small amounts exist naturally on the surface of most fruits and vegetables.

Garlic, Bee Pollen, Cabbage as sources of Friendly Flora

In the 1980's someone wrote that raw garlic kills off good intestinal bacteria. They offered no proof for the statement. I decided to find out for myself if garlic kills off yogurt cultures and did an experiment using a yogurt maker. After heating milk to near boiling temperature and then cooling it, I filled up 4 6 ounce jars. I added some chopped raw garlic to one milk container, a small amount of bee pollen to another and yogurt (with active cultures) to another and left one untreated as a control.

After 24 hours, the results came in. The one with the raw garlic formed a firm solid curd. The one with the bee pollen formed a solid curd and the one with the yogurt cultures added also formed a solid curd. The untreated jar was still liquid. The experiment was repeated again with the same results. The solid curd tasted like yogurt and had a lower pH value typical of yogurt. In other words, it had a tart taste and you could taste the lactic acid.

Conclusion: you can increase the friendly flora in your gut by eating some raw garlic or taking a few bee pollen capsules with each meal just as you can do so by using probiotic capsules. In Chapter 8, I tell you how to make cultured cabbage juice, another potent source of friendly flora containing some wild strains of L. Plantarum. Of course, if you cook everything before you eat it, you kill off the friendly flora in the food as well as the unfriendly like listeria and salmonella. Eggs, pork, and chickens produced in crowded farm factories are especially vulnerable to spreading infections like e-coli. Free range poultry and grass fed beef is healthier by far

In another experiment, I added some hydrogen peroxide to a jar of milk in the yogurt maker and it did not form a curd after 24 hours. It confirmed earlier reports that taking hydrogen peroxide orally is an antibiotic that will kill off friendly intestinal flora along with the unfriendly varieties. This raises a question about food preservatives and I did not test them individually. However, logic tells us that preservatives with antimicrobial properties will just as likely suppress the growth of friendly as unfriendly bacteria. Sodium benzoate and potassium sorbate are two common food preservatives, yet their effects on friendly flora have not been tested in a controlled experiment.

Published Scientific Research on Probiotics
The following excerpts are based on searches done at the United States National Library of Medicine (PubMed)

1. Antiallergic Effects of Probiotics, by Arthur Ouwehand (Journal of Nutrition -2004)

Page 1 *"Clinical trials have shown that the standard treatment of infants with atopic eczema,..... can be significantly improved through the addition of Lactobacillus rhamnosus GG or Bifidobacterium lactis Bb-12."*

Page 5 *"Prevention of allergic disease. In addition to treatment of allergy, it has been observed that selected probiotics can reduce the risk for the development of allergy."*

Page 6 *"Mechanisms by which probiotics may influence food allergy. 1) Improved mucosal barrier function. 2) Modulation of intestinal microbiota composition and activity. 3) Stimulated production of secretory IgA. 5) Change in mucus production. 6) Direct immune modulation."* (This article is supported with 36 footnotes referencing other articles at the NLM Pubmed)

2.. Heat-killed Lactobacillus Plantarum L-137 suppresses naturally fed antigen-specific IgE production by stimulation of IL-12 production in mice, by Murosaki S et al; J Allergy Clin Immunol, Jul 1998. (*"CONCLUSION: our results suggest that L. plantarum L-137, a potent IL-12 inducer, is useful for the prevention and treatment of food allergy."*)

3. Clinical Indications for Probiotics: an overview, by Goldin BR et al (Clin Infect Dis, Feb 1 2008)

Abstract: *"randomized double-blind studies have provided evidence of probiotic effectiveness for the treatment and prevention of acute diarrhea and antibiotic-induced diarrhea, a well as for the prevention of cow milk-induced allergy in infants and young children."*

4. Immunostimulatory oligodeoxynucleotide from B. longum suppresses Th2 immune responses in a murine model, by Takahashi N et al (Clin Exp Immunol Jul 2006)

Abstract: "….probiotics might be useful in preventing allergic disease."

5. Effect of oral probiotics administration on ovalbumin-induced food allergy mouse model, by Kim JY et al (J Microbiol Biotechnol Aug 2008)
Abstract: "The groups treated with probiotics had decreased levels of degranulated mast cell, eosinophil granules, and tail scabs. These results indicate that L. acidophilus AD031 and B. lactis AD011 might be useful for the prevention of allergy."

6. Improvements in seasonal allergic disease with Lactobacillus plantarum No. 14, by Nagata Y et al (Biosci Biotechnol Ciochem Sep 2010)
Abstract: " We conducted randomized, placebo-controlled, double-blind studies of Lactobacillus plantarum No. 14 (LP 14) in female students with seasonal allergic diseases…in the LP 14 group, the percentage of Th1 cells significantly increased."

7. Suppression of type-1 allergic responses by oral administration of grape marc fermented with Lactobacillus plantarum, by Tominaga T et al (Immuopharmacol Immunotoxicol Dec 2010)
Abstract: "These results indicate that oral administration of FGM, prepared from Koshu grape for white wine….. could suppress both phases of type-1 allergic responses."

8. Efficacy of Lactobacillus strain HSK201 in relief from Japanese cedar pollinosis, by Hasegawa T et al (Biosci Biotechnol Biochem Dec 2009)
Abstract: "Although this was a preliminary study with 19 employees of our own company serving as subjects, the results suggest that ingestions of the HSK201 strain (L. plantarum) alleviates pollinosis symptoms during the period when pollen exposure is low and the symptoms are mild."

9. Therapeutic advantages of medicinal herbs fermented with Lacto bacillus plantarum in topical application and its activities on atopic dermatitis, by Joo SS et al (Phytother Res Jul 2009)
Abstract: "The present study examined whether selected herbal extracts fermented in Lactobacillus plantarum (FHE) possesses anti-AD properties….. the results presented in this study suggest that FHE may have therapeutic advantages for the treatment of AD…"

10. Immunomodulatory properties of Lactobacillus plantarum and its use as a recombinant vaccine against mite allergy, by Rigaux P et al (Allergy Mar 2009)

Abstract: *"both wild-type or recombinant L. plantarum reduced airway eosinophilia following aerosolized allergen exposure and IL-5 secretion upon allergen stimulation….. L .plantarum producing Der P I represents a promising vaccine against house dust mite allergy."*

11. In vivo and in vitro immunomodulation of Der p I allergen-specific response by Lactobacillus plantarum bacteria, by Hisbergues M et al (Clin Exp Allergy Sep 2007)

12. Recombinant Lactobacillus plantarum inhibits house dust mite specific T-cell responses, by Kruisselbrink A et al (Clin Exp Immunol Oct 2001)

Abstract: *"recent evidence suggests that chronic exposure to lactobacilli, which are part of the normal intestinal flora, inhibits the development of allergic diseases….. these data suggests that recombinant L. plantarum may be a suitable candidate for the treatment of allergic disorders."*

13.. Inhibitory effect of Lactobacillus plantarum K-I on passive Cutaneous anaphylaxis reaction and scratching behavior in mice, by Jang S.E et al (Arch Pharm Res Dec 2011)

Abstract: *"Based on these findings, LP may improve allergic diseases such as anaphylaxis, atopic dermatitis, rhinitis and Pruritus…"*

14. Probiotics, prebiotics and synbiotics, by de Vrese M and Schreaenmeir J, (Adv Biochem Eng Bioechnol. 2008

Abstract: *"Well-established probiotic effects are …..6. Prevention or alleviation of allergies and atopic dermatitis in infants."*

Note - 7 categories of probiotic benefits were listed in this abstract.

L Acidophilus – an acid loving bacteria that converts sugars into lactic acid. Colonizes the mouth and intestinal tract and vagina. Creates an acidic environment that repels yeast and fungal infections.

Ref: **Acidophilus milk products: a review of potential benefits to consumers.** Gilliland SE. *J Dairy Sci.* 1989 Oct;72(10):2483

L Rhamnosus – especially beneficial in supporting immune responses to infectious diseases. Promotes immunity to colon cancer.

Ref: Enhancement of natural and acquired immunity by Lactobacillus rhamnosus (HN001), Lactobacillus acidophilus (HN017) and Bifidobacterium lactis (HN019). Gill HS, Rutherfurd KJ, Prasad J, Gopal PK. *Br J Nutr.* 2000 Feb;83(2):167-76.

L Plantarum – reduces food sensitivities, promotes Th1 cytokines and immunity to cancer.

Ref: Heat-killed Lactobacillus plantarum L-137 suppresses naturally fed antigen-specific IgE production by stimulation of IL-12 production in mice. Murosaki S, Yamamoto Y, Ito K, Inokuchi T, Kusaka H, Ikeda H, Yoshikai Y. *J Allergy Clin Immunol.* 1998 Jul;102(1):57-64.

Immunomodulatory effects of Lactobacillus plantarum on human colon cancer cells. Paolillo R, Romano Carratelli C, Sorrentino S, Mazzola N, Rizzo A. *Int Immunopharmacol.* 2009 Oct;9(11):1265-71. Epub 2009 Jul 29.

L Salivarius - helps with colitis and inflammation.

Ref: Selecting lactic acid bacteria for their safety and functionality by use of a mouse colitis model. Daniel C, Poiret S, Goudercourt D, Dennin V, Leyer G, Pot B. *Appl Environ Microbiol.* 2006 Sep;72(9):5799-805.

B. Bifidum- B. Bifidum reduces inflammatory reaction in the intestines, regulates components of the mucus membranes, and improves intestinal integrity.

Ref: Bifidobacterium bifidum improves intestinal integrity in a rat model of necrotizing enterocolitis. Khailova L, Dvorak K, Arganbright KM, Halpern MD, Kinouchi T, Yajima M, Dvorak B. *Am J Physiol Gastrointest Liver Physiol.* 2009 Nov;297(5):G940-9.

B Longum – Promotes IGA and anti-inflammatory cytokines.

Ref: Immunomodulatory impact of a symbiotic in T(h)1 and T(h)2 models of infection. Cazzola M, Tompkins TA, Matera MG. *Ther Adv Respir Dis.* 2010 Oct;4(5):259-70.

Chapter 6
Fiber and select foods that support the growth of friendly intestinal flora

Flaxseed

Cardio protective effects come from the alpha linolenic acid in flax oil - a type of Omega 3 fatty acid. Flaxseed oil reduces inflammation, triglycerides, is anti-thrombotic, anti-arrhythmic, inhibits nuclear factor kappa B activity, down regulates fatty acid synthesis, and up regulates fatty acid oxidation. (1)

Flaxseed proteins - Udenigwe CC and Aluko RE report on the antioxidant and ACE inhibitor found in flaxseed protein. Flax may help to normalize blood pressure, prevent or treat liver disease and oxidative stress. (2)

Flaxseed powder provides cardio protective benefits for 3 reasons. Flaxseed contains omega-3 fatty acids, dietary fiber and phytoestrogen lignans. Studies report that flaxseed consumed daily can reduce total cholesterol, LDL cholesterol, improves vascular relaxation and inhibits ventricular fibrillation. (3)

Flax seed also inhibits the cancer promoting effects of soy by modulating estrogen receptors. (5)

Higher bone density and treatment of renal (kidney) injury was reported in experiments on rats. (6)

Flaxseed has anti-oxidant restoration and enzyme liver protection benefits. Flaxseed meal at 5% of diet restored catalase, SOD and peroxidase by 39%, 181% and 123%, respectively. (7) Anti-Tumor effects of a lignans found in flaxseed in experiments on rats reduced tumor formation by 46%.(8)

French and Canadian researchers in separate studies found that flaxseed compounds suppress breast cancer cell growth. Researchers at the University of Picardie Jules Verne in Amiens, France isolated two lignans from flaxseeds and tested their effects on breast cell cancer lines MCF-7 and MDA-MB-231. The lignans isolated were secoisolariciresinol diglucoside (SDG) and anhydrosecoisolariciresinal, the latter decreased cell growth at 50 and 100 microM (9). Canadian researchers found that SDG, a lignan in flax seeds, reduced tumor cell proliferation growth and the flax oil also inhibited growth. (10)

This and other studies suggest that the anticancer properties of flax come from both the extracted oil and the lignans in the seeds. The results of various studies suggest that there would be an added benefit from using both flaxseed oil and flaxseed powder. Since the oil is in whole freshly ground flaxseed powder, using 2 tablespoon of flaxseed powder in vegetable or fruit juice 2 or 3 times a day for adults seems like an essential component of an anti-cancer program. For prevention: 1 Tbsp daily of ground flaxseed powder daily.

Note: in the original Gerson Cancer treatments, 1 Tbsp of freshly pressed flaxseed oil was mixed with nonfat yogurt and consumed twice a day along with a glass of freshly pressed organic apple and carrot juice, given each hour throughout the day.

Psyllium husks - Scientific research

Researchers have found that psyllium husk powder will reduce cholesterol levels, the body mass index, as well as, both systolic and diastolic blood pressure in studies. Psyllium also significantly reduced triglyceride levels in the blood. (1) Studies on calves fed psyllium as part of their diet had an increase in the mass of digested foods in the duodenum, jejunem, and colon. (2) The intestinal tissues had about a 25% increase in density indicating a stronger gastro-intestinal tract. The researchers reported that: "Supplementation of psyllium to milk replacer increased fermentation in the colon, mass of the total GIT, populations of bifido-bacteria, and lactobacilli in the reticulo-rumen." (2)

It should also be noted that researchers have found that inhalation of psyllium seed powder (not the husks) has been associated with asthma. (3) In trying any new fiber product, always consider the possibility of a food sensitivity or inflammatory immune response in the form of an allergic or hypersensitivity reaction, or a rash as a topical skin reaction.

HIGH FIBER DIET PROMOTES ACIDOPHILUS AND BIFIDO BACTERIA

Published research has found that a diet high in fiber (30 to 35 grams daily) progressively lowers the pH of the colon (14) and significantly increases butyrate levels. The butyrate is produced by bifidus and bifido-bacteria (B Longum) from undigested carbohydrates in the bran.

Dr. Sehnert MD reports that acidophilus produces B-complex vitamins including folic acid, niacin, B6, B12, riboflavin, biotin, and pantothenic acid (15). He also reports that acidophilus produces lactase enzyme that digests lactose in milk and inhibits the growth of Candida Albicans. David Webster writes "a floating stool is often an indicator of the existence of a predominately acidophilus flora."(13)

Pectin promotes friendly flora, shrinks tumors, and reduces lead levels

Pectin is a soluble fiber found in many fruits and vegetables especially apples, citrus rinds, cranberries, quince, peas, beans, and legumes. Pectin helps reduces triglycerides and other fatty components in the blood. Researchers in Japan found that eating two apples a day increased the number of lactobacillus and bifido-bacteria in the fecal samples tested and also decreased the pH of the stool while reducing the amount of ammonia present. They concluded that eating apples improved the intestinal environment. (1)

Researchers in Florida tested quercitin, a plant flavinoid and citrus pectin, on colon solid tumor implants on bald mice. Modified forms of quercitin and citrus pectin were used in the study. After 20 days, they concluded that: *A significant reduction in tumor size was noted at day 20 in all groups compared to controls. The groups given low-dose QC and MCP had a 29-percent (NS) and 38-percent (p<0.02) decrease in size, respectively."* (2)

In experiments on children, researchers found that modified citrus pectin reduced the lead levels in blood serum. They found in an increase in lead levels in the urine of the same children given the citrus pectin. They stated: *"The need for a gentle, safe heavy metal-chelating agent, especially for children with high environmental chronic exposure, is great. The dramatic results and no observed adverse effects in this pilot study along with previous reports of the safe and effective use of MCP in adults indicate that MCP could be such an agent."* (3)

Based on my own experience, I would not make any fiber formula with less than 3% or more than 10% pectin by weight. This allows it to disperse in the stomach without causing any discomfort. Sources: Pectin powder without sugar is sold in stores.

1. **Effect of apple intake on fecal microbiota and metabolites in humans;** Shinohara K, Ohashi Y, Kawasumi K, Terada A, Fujisawa T.; *Anaerobe.* 2010 Oct;16(5):510-5. Epub 2010 Mar 19.
2.**Effects of daily oral administration of quercetin chalcone and modified citrus pectin on implanted colon-25 tumor growth in Balb-c mice.** Hayashi A, Gillen AC, Lott JR. *Altern Med Rev.* 2000 Dec;5(6):546-52.
3.   **The role of modified citrus pectin as an effective chelator of lead in children hospitalized with toxic lead levels.** Zhao ZY, Liang L, Fan X, Yu Z, Hotchkiss AT, Wilk BJ, Eliaz I. *Altern Ther Health Med.* 2008 Jul-Aug;14(4):34-8. Altern Ther Health Med. 2008 Nov-Dec;14(6):18. Department of Medicine, Children's Hospital, Zhejiang University School of Medicine, Hangzhou, Republic of China.

Glucomannan nourishes bifidobacteria increases HDL - lowers triglycerides

Research indicates that glucomannan; a fiber from the Konjac root, strongly supports the growth of bifidobacteria, as does FOS. Degradation of glucomannan by enzymes and friendly flora in human feces has produced formic acid, acetic acid, proprionic acid and 1-butyric acid. (27) Other researchers have found that glucomannan increases the good HDL cholesterol and lowers triglycerides (28)

Chicory Inulin and FructoOligoSaccharides (FOS)

FOS and inulin, indigestible carbohydrates, are found in artichokes, chicory, whole rye, bananas, onions, garlic, and asparagus. They are potent fertilizers to promote the growth of both bifidus and acidophilus in the large intestines. There is some distrust among health professionals of using FOS made through the enzymatic processing of white sugar.

On FOS, Martin Feldman MD states:

"FOS passes through the system with minimal problems and a low incidence of intolerant or allergic reactions. It is of interest that the digestive system does not break down FOS. Rather, it reaches the lower intestines intact, where it is devoured by the "friendly bacteria" without significantly assisting the "unfriendly bacteria." These properties make FOS extremely beneficial in treating a variety of digestive problems." (16)

Other benefits of good flora like B Longum and bifidus are increased absorption of calcium, magnesium and iron as well as other nutrients. It is the butyric acid produced by the bifidobacteria that rebuilds the mucus membranes and heals leaky gut syndrome, a condition directly linked to allergies, multiple chemical sensitivity, chronic fatigue, systemic candidiasis, depression, various skin problems, loss of mental clarity, and eye floaters.

To grow a healthy garden, it takes good soil, good seed, and fertilizer. Our internal garden in the colon, to be healthy, depends on fiber (the soil), indigestible carbohydrates (FOS or inulin - the fertilizer) and probiotics (the seed). The Japanese have been ahead of the Americans in many areas of health for decades. They have used FOS in their foods since 1983 along with bifidobacteria and omega 3 fatty acids from seaweed.

A search of the medical literature finds no toxic or mutagenic effects even from very large doses of FOS in both animals and humans. Here is a summary of a wide range of benefits being reported in the literature on FOS.

1. Significantly increases the presence of bifidus, B Longum, bifidobacteria (various strains) and acidophilus noticeable 6 days after ingestion of FOS begins.

2. Significantly lowers the pH of the colon and the feces (reportedly to less than 6.0).

3. Reduces toxins in the stools from unfriendly flora.

4. Reduces production of fat by the liver (lowers the bad LDL cholesterol).

5. **Significantly increases the absorption of calcium, magnesium and iron** (indicating benefits for persons affected by insomnia, poor digestion, osteoporosis, and anemia).

6. Produces short chain fatty acids in the large intestines.

34

7. Significantly increases butyric acid production (reverses mucosal atrophy, rebuilds the mucus membranes and heals a leaky gut) - this will be of immediate benefit to persons with allergies, MCS, candidiasis and cancer.

8. Reduces free radicals and oxidative stress (should help increase Glutathione levels, the cells main antioxidant used against free radicals and for processing antigen) - thus improving CD8 cytotoxic lymphocyte activity against intracellular infections.

9. Potential health benefits reported (short list) as reducing the risk of colon cancer, non-insulin-type diabetes, obesity, osteoporosis and cancer.

10. Protects the liver against many toxins. Reduces the toxins of ammonia and amines in the feces.

11. Increases mucosal surface to improve nutrient absorption. Nutrient transport across the epithelium is aided by an increase in calcium in the mucosal membranes.

12. In animal experiments, FOS inhibited the growth of breast cancer and other tumors.

13. Promotes B vitamin production by bifidobacteria.

Food Sources of FOS

Contrary to the wide spread belief that FOS will feed the growth of Candida and Klebsiella, I have found no scientific proof or lab tests from individuals to substantiate this. Yet, anecdotal reports suggest that a person who has high levels of candida albicans or Klebsiella may be better off obtaining their FOS from whole food sources. I have yet to find a person with either of these conditions who cannot tolerate **onions, asparagus, or artichokes**, foods that are all very high in FOS.

Tolerance of food sources of FOS could be because other factors like sulfur are present in onions and asparagus that kill off intestinal pathogens and may be suppressing the candida and Klebsiella while the FOS increases the growth of the bifido-bacteria. **For sensitive persons, using whole foods high in FOS might be a better initial choice than using FOS as a dietary supplement.** If desired, FOS as a supplement can always be added later on.

Chapter 7
How to promote probiotic growth

A Perfect Stool Formula

When seeking a fiber supplement, look for a premixed multi-fiber and multi-probiotic blend. This gives the best results in terms of obtaining normal bowel movements and maximizing the growth of intestinal flora. **Avoid fiber blends with bentonite,** a drawing clay as **it is too harsh for continuous use** and if you have a sensitive digestive tract, it will make it more sore and sensitive. Bentonite will aggravate an ulcer or irritable bowel.

The following formula is a gentle formula you can make on you own that has produced excellent results for hundreds of people over the past decade:

1. 16 ozs flaxseed powder or psyllium husk powder of a 50/50 mixture of both.
2. Eight ounces of chicory inulin (Cargill Oligo-Instant) or FOS
3. Two ounces of pectin – plain unsweetened.
4. Two ounces of glucomannan (Konjac) powder
5. Four to eight ounces of a probiotic blend (L Acidophilus, L rhamnosus, B longum, B bifidus, L plantarum and others if desired)

Mix all ingredients together and place in a freezer. Remove a pint of the mixture and keep in the refrigerator. Mix one tablespoon with a glass of water or fruit juice and take 1 or 2 times daily before meals. Results are noticeable in a few days (no more constipation, easy bowel movements, large diameter stools, normal brown appearance, low odor, semi soft, floats on water)

Note: I have had good results with a premixed fiber and probiotics blend called Colon Comfort Formula that is distributed to health food stores. (Ojibwa Tea of Life, Denver CO 303-322-7930)

Probiotics that protect against candida albicans

Acidophilus lives primarily in the small intestines while bifidus, B. Longum and other bifidobacteria reside primarily in the large intestines. Wagner et al found that 4 strains of probiotics all significantly reduced the presence of candida albicans when fed to immunodeficient mice. (23). The 4 strains were **L. acidophilus, L reuteri, L casei and B animalis.** Wagner reported that the probiotics protected the mice against fungal infections by both immunological and non-immunologic mechanisms.

In animal experiments, Rani B et al found that when a food mixture of millet flour, chickpea flour, skim milk and tomato pulp was pre-fermented with L acidophilus for 24 hours before being fed to mice that it inhibited the growth of pathogenic organisms (22).

Scientists in the Netherlands discover that Calcium stimulates acidophilus growth

Persons with chronic yeast infections consistently report that stool sample analysis finds no acidophilus present. This happens in spite of the fact that these people daily consume large amounts of yogurt and acidophilus supplements. Is there something in the intestines that is killing off the acidophilus? Are the candida albicans killing the acidophilus? Is their some internal or external toxin destroying the acidophilus?

In March, 1999, an article published in the Journal of Nutrition (24) by Bovee-Oudenhoven and three other researchers found that in experiments in rats that giving calcium phosphate as a dietary supplement increased acidophilus growth in both infected (with salmonella) and non-infected rats.

The researchers found that certain substances present in bile, kill acidophilus in the small intestines and cited the work of several other researchers to support their observations. In the course of digestion, the liver sends bile into the small intestines to digest fat. However, the liver also dumps toxins in the bile at the same time. These toxins in the bile have been found to kill off the friendly acidophilus that predominately like to reside in the small intestines. The researchers stated:

"Besides reducing the cytotoxicity of the ileal (small intestine) and the concentration of the bile acids and fatty acids of ileal contents and fecal water, calcium phosphate notably changed the composition of the ileal bile acids in a less cell-damaging direction.... significantly greater numbers of ileal and fecal

lactobacilli were detected in non-infected, calcium phosphate supplements rats."

The researchers found that calcium phosphate not only precipitated the toxic substances out of the bile but actually reduced the amount of bile as well. These actions suggest to me that calcium phosphate's action might have been on the liver as a detoxifying agent. If the liver has fewer toxins, then it should produce bile with fewer toxins. However, a second factor emerges: if the rats eat less fat, the liver will also produce less bile.

Another source of natural calcium is **low fat plain yogurt**. Calcium is also found in **bone meal** although with the occasional scare of mad cow disease, a better and safer choice is **Coral calcium** that comes from the Coral reef near Okinawa, Japan.

Two forms of calcium have been identified that are the result of normal digestion with wholesome foods: they are calcium phosphate and calcium sulfate. While **IP6 (inositol hexaphosphate)** promotes calcium phosphate, another substance called **inositol hexasulfate (IS6)** helps increase calcium sulfate levels, (another of the 12 essential cell salts). IS6, like IP6 (phytic acid) are natural substances found in whole grains.

Natural Selenium supports immune responses

Two types of white bloods cells, macrophages and neutrophils, are very important for controlling candida albicans and other fungal infections. In the United Kingdom at the Univ of Oxford, P Eggleton found that IP6 enhanced the *"phagocytosis by neutrophils in the presence of microbial stimuli."* (26). Plant based selenium (Phytosel, Sel-Broc, or yeast based) enhances neutrophil activity and increases glutathione levels in white blood cells. Selenium has strong protective effects against all types of cancer. Brazil Nuts are the richest known natural source of Selenium. Suggested amount for adults: Eat 2 to 4 Brazil nuts daily. This will provide about 200 to 400 mcg of natural selenium.

Another immune modulator is IP6. It is reported in medical journals to activate natural killer cells; defend against many types of cancer (Colon, Fibrosarcoma, Liver, Lung, Breast and skin), dissolves kidney stones, dissolves calcium deposits in the arteries (hardening of), antioxidant (prevents lipid peroxidation), prevents strokes, heart attacks, lowers triglycerides and cholesterol and is involved in normalizing many metabolic processes inside the cells. Adult dose suggested is 1000 mg per 25 lbs of body weight or about 6000 mg daily taken between meals in divided doses.

Lemon Juice promotes probiotic growth

Most varieties of commercial yogurt are made with 3 strains of flora. They are S. Thermophilus, L Bulgaricus, and Acidophilus. Recently, my attempts to make yogurt without Thermophilus and Bulgaricus added ended in failure until I made an important discovery. By adding 1 tsp. of lemon juice to a 6 ounce glass of milk, I could produce a solid curd in milk in a yogurt maker in 24 hours using only the strains of acidophilus, bifidus and B Longum from a capsule. Previous attempts to do this ended in failure.

The yogurt I made by adding lemon juice and these 3 strains has a very sour taste and a low pH of 4.5. The original milk had a pH of 6.4. When I added 1 tsp. of lemon juice, the pH of the milk dropped to 5.5. After 24 hours of culturing, it dropped further to 4.5. Now this is real sour and very healthy yogurt teeming with tens of billions of acidophilus.

Now it seems reasonable that the same thing could happen with a meal if you take the juice of half a lemon with each meal and take along with it your acidophilus supplements. The fermentation process would start in the stomach and continue into the small and large intestines. By using lemon juice with foods high in calcium plus the acidophilus cultures, we may at last have discovered the secret of successfully implanting this most valuable strain of friendly flora. Controlled studies of stool samples of persons using lemon juice and calcium-rich foods or supplements still needs to be done to confirm that this is the breakthrough I believe it is.

Summary of foods, nutrients and supplements that support the growth of probiotics

1. Lemon Juice used with meals and probiotic supplements. Two tablespoons of lemon juice may be sprinkled over food or placed in a glass of water to which you add 1/2 tsp of acidophilus powder or take 2 capsules.

2. Foods high in calcium. Canned salmon, sardines, kelp, seaweed, spirulina, wheat grass, barley grass, kamut grass, blackstrap molasses, tofu, winter squash, pumpkin, carrots, buckwheat, cabbage, and all dark green leafy vegetables - kale, endive, parsley, collard greens, spinach, romaine lettuce etc. Whole foods are your best source of calcium and minerals.

Products that deplete calcium and other minerals from the body are sugar and corn syrup and refined sweeteners found in many processed foods (i.e. soda, colas, etc, candy, cakes and other refined carbohydrates, also hard liquor, but not beer when used in moderation).

3. Foods naturally high in inulin and/or FOS - onions, asparagus, artichokes, and garlic.

4. Probiotics – L acidophilus, L rhamnosus, L salivarius, L plantarum, B longum and B bifidum are a good mix to promote intestinal health and mucosal immunity.

5. Biotin - a B vitamin - best used with L glutamine.

6. Supplements: Ip6 a source of both calcium and magnesium phosphate. **Coral Calcium,** derived from the Coral reef, has about 70 trace minerals included, some of which help with the utilization of calcium within the body. Although in the carbonate form, there are credible widespread reports on the health benefits of Coral calcium. Use IP6 or Coral Calcium between meals or on an empty stomach. I personally found that Coral Calcium dissolved a bone spur in my foot and helps me sleep deeper at night. [*I did not get any of these benefits from my previous use of liquid calcium supplements or calcium citrate.*]

Ip6 and Coral calcium are both derived from natural sources and have a proven track record of efficacy in helping to dissolve bad calcium, improving immune function and increase bone density. You can't say all these benefits occur for liquid calcium supplements and numerous other manufactured calcium products that are widely marketed. Some of these products I believe, actually create other mineral imbalances if they are used long-term

7. Selenium – best natural source is Brazil Nuts followed by seafoods. Avoid synthetic forms of selenium like L. selenomethionine – a man made version that has had adverse effects with no solid research data that supports it efficacy.

Snack suggestion: Use raw garlic plus acidophilus/B longum capsules or powder with each meal. Sprinkle the probiotic powder over your food. Except for foods high in FOS, raw vegetables promote acidophilus growth better than cooked vegetables. With foods high in FOS (onions, artichokes, and asparagus), eating them cooked works just as well as eating them raw. Try a clove of garlic sliced on rye crisp with marinated artichokes or, if you cannot tolerate raw garlic, try spreading plain yogurt on rye crisp and top it with marinated artichokes.

For breakfast; 1. buckwheat pancakes with strawberry yogurt. 2. a poached egg on whole grain gluten-free bread that you "butter" with plain yogurt. 3. Cooked millet, whole cornmeal, quinoa or brown rice cereal topped with a fruit flavored yogurt and sliced bananas (high in FOS). If you use soy milk, mix in one tablespoon of yogurt and shake in a jar. If you do not eat yogurt, take a probiotic with both acidophilus and B longum in it.

Do not use soy or rice milk with "carrageenan" added. Carageenan suppresses immune function by inhibiting macrophage activity. Consider brands that leave out the carrageenan.

Avoid cold processed breakfast cereals. **In an animal experiment, processed "cold" cereal bran caused more cancer than the control diet**. Beware of all precooked foods that are currently on the market. All foods cooked at temperatures above 400° F are unsafe for human consumption. Foods that are boiled or cooked in a Crock Pot at temperatures at or below the boiling temperature of water are very safe to eat.

41

Chapter 8
The Miracle of Cultured Cabbage Juice

To help heal damaged mucus membranes of the G.I. tract, you need to drink about 1 and 1/2 cup daily of cultured cabbage juice. Here is how to make it. Fill a blender with chopped green cabbage and add spring water until about 2/3 full. Beat at high speed in the blender for one minute. Pour mixture into a bowl and repeat with two more batches. Cover with Saran wrap or similar material and let stand at room temperature. After 3 days, the cabbage juice solution is ready to use. Strain the mixture to separate the liquid from the pulp. Place the cultured cabbage juice in a refrigerator. Drink 1/2 cup of this solution diluted with an equal part of water 2 or 3 times each day. When your supply gets low, make a second batch just like the first one, except, and add 1/2 cup of the juice from the first batch to the second bath. Your second batch will be ready in just 24 hours.

The lactic acid in the cultured cabbage juice will purify the G.I. tract and kill most strains of fungi, parasites and other pathogens.

You should drink this mixture until your stools float and are low odor. You can also obtain benefit from eating raw cabbage or coleslaw. Sauerkraut juice sold in the store is very beneficial for all kinds of intestinal infections and problems. Drink 4 ounces three times a day.

Miracle foods to heal a sore G.I. tract

1. **Pureed vegetables raw or cooked mixed with plain yogurt and a little flaxseed oil.** Add 1 TBSP flax oil to 8 ounces on non-fat yogurt. Mix one cup of baby food or raw pureed vegetables with one-half cup of the yogurt-flax oil mixture. Eat slowly every hour or two throughout the day.

2. **Pumpkin-** make a filling using coconut milk in place of cow's milk

3. **Squash** – cut in half bake face down with a little added. Add some butter and a little maple syrup. (Consider Squash soup made with coconut milk)

4. **Sweet potatoes** – Bake for 45 minutes - season same as squash.

5. **Okra** – soothing to the intestines

6. **Raw potato slices** eaten slowly (heals ulcers and colon inflammation)

7. **L-glutamine – use as directed.**

8. **Oatmeal water** – a rich natural source of beta glucan, an immune booster. Make by adding ½ cup of whole oats or rolled oats to a quart of spring water and refrigerate it for 24 hours. Strain and drink ½ cup every hour or two.

Meal Suggestions

For breakfast, see the suggestions at the end of the last chapter.
LUNCH:

Main meal: Raw Salad- endive, parsley, beet greens, romaine lettuce, sliced onions, garlic, carrots, artichokes, avocado, tomatoes, cucumbers, broccoli or red cabbage, red or yellow peppers and most any other vegetable. You can also add ripe olives, hot peppers and low sodium feta cheese, cottage cheese or plain yogurt. (Soak the feta cheese in a dish of water for one hour. This removes most of the sodium from the cheese). Top the salad with flavored vinegar like Balsamic vinegar and a good quality Extra Virgin Olive oil plus a little oregano. Use Sea Salt if you need more flavor.

Note: Fresh refrigerated flax oil 1 or 2 teaspoons may be mixed with the nonfat yogurt or cottage cheese. Use this mixture as a vegetable dip. Serve the salad with a whole grain bread that is high in fiber. Go to your health food store and find a bread that has 4 grams of fiber per slice. Eat 2 slices with this meal. This meal will add 12 to 14 grams of fiber to your daily diet. Now you should have reached the daily recommended dose of 27 to 29 grams of fiber. Congratulations! You are on our way to a new healthier body. **Sources of IP6:** Whole kernel corn or cornbread made from whole kernel ground corn, brown and wild rice and whole grain breads.

Proteins sources: 1. Cooked brown and wild rice flavored by adding the seaweed Kombu and a little red pepper and curry powder while cooking it. 2. **Canned salmon** or sardines, especially **"spiced sardines."** 3. **Sunflower seeds over mashed potatoes**

with plain yogurt. 4. Chicken or turkey cooked in a Crock Pot for 6 hours at 175°F. After cooking in a Crock Pot, chicken or turkey can be stored in refrigerator and sliced over a salad. It is very important to avoid any foods cooked at a temperature over 350°F. It is far healthier to cook meats at below the boiling temperature of water. They are far easier to digest.

FOS: Onions - baked or French Onion soup and artichokes are your two most potent sources. Also consider garlic and asparagus. Fruits: bananas contain FOS.

Main Meals: cooked. Boiled, simmered or cooked in a Crock Pot only for several hours at about 175°F. You can mix chicken or turkey with several vegetables like celery, carrots, onions, potatoes, brown and wild rice etc. and cook them all together. Avoid pork, ham, sausage or smoked foods. Once a week try a beef pot roast or brisket. Serve with horseradish. Good choices (think orange): cooked squash, sweet potatoes, yams, carrots and pumpkin. Tofu, split green or yellow pea soup, lentil soup.

Buckwheat muffins: Add one cup of canned pumpkin to the batter before baking. Buckwheat supports the growth of both acidophilus and bifidus as well as kidney function.

Steamed onions, carrots and cabbage as a side dish.

Homemade vegetable soups with chicken, turkey, and beef added are good choices.

Avoid eating sweet fruits and vegetables together as this can cause digestive problems and gas. The exception is lemons, limes, grapefruit, raw pineapple and natural applesauce. Most other sweet fruits should be eaten alone. Regarding pea soup, peas and chickpeas, test these out and see how your stomach can handle them before making them a daily course. Except for cottage cheese, cheese made from rice or soy is easier to digest than cheese made from cow's milk. Also, traces of rennet (enzymes to curdle milk) in hard cheese (cheddar etc) can cause muscle cramps and rheumatoid arthritis.

Detoxify with the whole Lemon/Olive oil drink

Whole Lemon/Olive Oil drink. Several persons have reported that the daily use of this drink helps them sleep like a baby. The drink is made by taking the juice of one whole lemon and place it in a blender. Add cut up pieces of half a lemon rind with the seeds removed. Add a small piece of fresh ginger root (about one inch) and a glass of water or fruit juice (i.e. red grape is a good choice or use filtered water if you have an active yeast infection). Add 1 tablespoon of cold pressed Extra Virgin Olive Oil and blend for 2 minutes. Drink the whole thing, pulp and all the liquid. Once a day is suggested or less often if desired. The pulp has fiber and pectin so it is beneficial to consume it all. This drink will help remove heavy metals, detoxify the liver and lymph system and normalize saliva pH at a normal 6.4. If the saliva pH is low or acid after using the drink for a week, it is important to take a food-based calcium supplement like coral calcium and/or increase your intake of dark green vegetables and even soft cooked fish bones found in sardines and salmon.

The best supplements are from whole foods

The best supplements are made by Nature or by the hand of God. They are more effective in promoting balance in metabolism and in the immune system than many products that isolate the "active" ingredient only to discover years later that the other factors that are ignored in these whole foods were really important after all. Avoid mega dosing on vitamins. This will cause imbalances elsewhere in the body. It is time to get back to basics and Mother Nature.

Vitamin A and D - Cod liver oil - 1 to 3 teaspoons. daily - use the plain, not the emulsified. **Sun tanning** outdoors or inside in a tanning salon is a great way to increase Vitamin D production and thus calcium absorption.

B Complex vitamins – Max Stress B, Natural B vitamins or Brewer's yeast tablets.

Vitamin C - Rose hips or Acerola cherries - powder, tablets, extract or tea. Try Thayer's Slippery Elm lozenges, and rosehip lozenges or Nature's Answer alcohol free rose hip extract.

Vitamin E - raw wheat germ - vacuum packed or nitrogen packed to ensure freshness. Refrigerate after opening.

Minerals – Coral Calcium **(for calcium, and trace minerals), Seawater concentrate** with the sodium removed and blackstrap molasses. **Kelp, Spirulina, Chlorella and seaweed** are great food sources of minerals. Mineral supplements like coral calcium should be taken at night while natural food-based vitamins are best taken in the morning. For **selenium – use Brazil nuts.**

Whole foods offer more in the way of duplicating the natural process, and provide most of the trace minerals and other factors we need in nutrition. "Manufactured supplements" with laboratory made vitamins in them have not been proven in scientific studies to match the safety and effectiveness of plant-based vitamins. Most vitamins, including amino acid chelates, sold today are not plant-based but are synthesized in a laboratory. Do not expect to see the word "synthetic" on the bottle. Marketers are cleaver enough to make their products appear "natural" often by mixing some natural ingredients with the synthetic and marketing it as "natural."

Raw vegetables that are high in carotenoids, calcium and FOS should be made part of the daily diet. They support the growth of both acidophilus and bifido-bacteria. Brewers yeast is an excellent source of natural selenium plus RNA and DNA, the building blocks of new cells. Brazil nuts each contain about 100 mcg of natural selenium. I would not use a selenium supplement containing "L-selenomethionine" as this is a man made amino acid complex. In 14 cases I have followed, this form of synthetic selenium provided no noticeable benefits and produced adverse side effects at over 400 mcg daily. High selenium yeast or plant based selenium (phytosel from Indian Mustard Greens)_are the most bioavailable and effective forms.

Selenium supplements that are solely plant derived are providing excellent results without adverse effects even when taken at higher doses of 800 mcg daily over extended periods of time (2 to 3 years). These include Phytosel, a trade name of Nucycle, manufacturers of Phytosel from hydroponicly greenhouse grown Indian Mustard Greens. It is an 100% plant based selenium. Selenium from yeast is also a good choice although not expected to produce a 100% plant based product (usually 90 to 95% is yeast based). Selenium promotes Neutrophil function, a type of white blood cell, that in turn helps to control yeast and fungal infections. Four Brazil Nuts daily also provide about 400 mcg of natural selenium.

Chapter 9
Specific Symptoms & Remedies

Acid-Reflux syndrome (heartburn)

Research published in Sept 2010 Lukic M et al in the Journal of Coll Antropol found in one study that smoking cigarettes, alcohol consumption (hard liquor), highly spiced foods, very hot foods, and/or fast eating with poor chewing (mastication) habits were the preferred eating habits of people with heartburn as compared to controls.

In London, Moazzaz R et al reported in the J Dental Research in Nov 2005 that sugar-free chewing gum reduced acid reflux and stomach acidity in a number of test subjects. The researchers stated that "Chewing sugar-free gum for half an hour after a meal can reduce acidic postprandial esophageal reflux." Use Xylitol based sugar free gum. Avoid the neurotoxin – aspartame. The use of apple cider vinegar or lemon juice has helped many people with acid-reflux condition. Try one tablespoon in water before each meal.

Diets high in fat, salt, and certain spices, chemical additives in food, tobacco smoke, (containing 7000 chemicals), smoke flavoring added to foods are major known irritant sources that also promotes acid-reflux. In reaction to chemical irritants and food sensitivities, mast cells in the gut mucosal produce type 2 histamine that in turn stimulate the production of more stomach acid. (1, 2) What the body seems to be telling us in acid reflux disease is that because some thing in the stomach is irritating to the surface cells, the stomach produces acid to destroy the "irritant."

Unwanted byproducts of digestion, called antigens, can also trigger an immune response that increases histamine production. Histamines are produced by mast cells that are found in the mucus membranes of the gut and also by a certain type of white blood cell (Basophils).

While over the counter products like Zantac, Pepcid, Tagamet and others can block excess histamine production (known as H2 blockers) and thus lower acid production in the stomach, the underlying cause of excess histamine production that is chemical additives and food allergies remains untreated. Products like

calcium carbonate, magnesium oxide, or baking soda directly lower stomach acid but do not reduce histamine levels. A better choice would be Coral Calcium powder that includes all the trace minerals– try 1/2 tsp with a glass of water when acid reflux is noticeable.

Homeopathic remedies: Calcium phosphate (Cal Phos) and Sodium Phosphate (Nat Phos). Take 4 to 8 tablets under the tongue until relief is obtained.

For the cure, you will need to eat a bland diet, avoid restaurant and processed foods, quit the smoking habit, and also avoid the use of hard liquor: A natural beer (Weiss) once in a while should be OK. Low fat, no fried foods, no ham, brats, hot dogs, no lunchmeat of any kind, few or no spices, low salt, no white bread, canned soda or refined carbohydrates. Drink more spring or artesian water. Avoid taking aspirin. Aspirin reduces the production of mucin, a component of intestinal mucus.

Diet must be high in fiber, low in fat, include raw and/or steamed vegetables, foods with FOS to support the growth of acidophilus and bifido-bacteria (B longum). Fermented foods like sauerkraut will help. Avoid stress. Be tested for food allergies and avoid the most offending foods. The dumbest thing anyone can do is to listen to the advertisers on TV who tell you to take over the counter treatments (the purple pills) and then to eat all the offending foods you want. That is a prescription for all kinds of intestinal problem including cancer down the road.

Allergies and food sensitivities

There are several ways of reducing food sensitivities and intolerances. A.) Avoidance – avoid the offending food. B.) A rotation diet is where you eat the offending food only once every 4 or 5 days. See the book on "The Rotation Diet." C.) Increase hydrochloric acid (HCL) in the stomach by supplementing with natural B vitamins to increase the bodies production of HCL or take HCL capsules. An alternative to HCL is to squeeze lemon juice over your foods or to use apple cider vinegar with meals. D.) Eat enzyme rich foods like raw ginger, raw pineapple, raw celery, and kiwi to improve digestion of proteins. E.) Cultured foods like sauerkraut works wonders. F.) The use of certain probiotics like L rhamnosus and L plantarum have been shown in scientific studies to reduce not only food allergies but allergies from multiple sources including tree, grass pollen and animal dander.

L. Plantarum and **L. Rhamnosus** can be used to reduce food allergies and sensitivities and these effects are well documented by published research. See Chapter 5. Anyone suffering from sinus or chest infections, asthma, COPD, and food allergies would most likely benefit from the use of these two probiotics.

Another method of desensitization is called NAET. Dr. Devi S Nambudripad is the discoverer and developer of the Nambudripad Allergy Elimination Technique or NAET. Various tests are available to detect allergies to food and environmental substances. These tests include the "Intra-dermal test," "patch test," "RAST" and "Eliza." These tests can identify dozens of allergens, substances that produce allergic reactions.

The NAET method of allergy elimination came to my attention from several persons with Chronic Fatigue Syndrome who reported good results for both food allergies and chemical sensitivities. Some people claim to permanently eliminate specific allergies with just one treatment. Others have had to repeat treatments several times for more stubborn allergic conditions. Dr. Nambudripad developed the technique that she first used on herself to eliminate her own allergies.

More information on the NAET treatment and a list of local health care practitioners trained in this technique can be obtained at this website on the internet: **www.naet.com** or you can write to NAET, 6714 Beach Blvd, Buena Park, CA 90621 Fax No 714-523-3068. Ph no 714-523-0800 or 523-8900

Appetite – how to stimulate

A loss of appetite is usually caused by a buildup of too many toxins in the liver, blood, colon, and lymph. Consider doing a liver flush - **the whole lemon/olive oil drink once daily** and drink lots of mineral rich spring water. (Do not drink distilled or reverse osmosis water as it is too acid and will leach minerals from the body). Before meals consider trying one or more of the following to increase your appetite.

1. **Cayenne**
2. **Apple cider vinegar**

3. **Blackstrap molasses – one teaspoon in glass of warm water before each meal.**
4. **Horseradish – put some on boiled cabbage r carrots.**
5. **Fasting** - drink mineral rich spring or artesian water and do not eat until you feel real hunger pangs in your stomach.
6. **Exercise – walk one half hour or more before each meal or after a meal.**
7. **Herbs**: Gentian root (Herbal Bitters), Ginger root (for digestion, of meats, nausea and to stop gas), Yam root extract or Oregon grape rooT.

If all else fails to promote your appetite, make yourself a cup of Marijuana tea using a pinch of the herb until you get a feel for its potency. It is not necessary to smoke it to get its benefits. Marinol capsules are also available with a prescription.

Cancer

Both L Plantarum and L Rhamnosus these should be used with meals and a high fiber diet as part of a cancer prevention program. B Longum that increases IgA is also very beneficial. This triple combination along with an anti-cancer diet like the one designed by Dr Max Gerson MD will maximize benefits to prevent cancer from occurring or reoccurring. Go to **gerson.org** for more information.

Candidiasis (yeast and fungal infections)

Most of the methods of treating chronic yeast infections focus on various methods of killing the yeast and eliminating carbohydrates and sugar from the diet. The problem with these methods is that alone they often do not bring a cure. The severe demands on dietary restrictions leave a person affected by candidiasis feeling trapped and deprived of many of simple joys of life like eating a piece of ripe fruit or having a hot fudge sundae or a bottle of beer.

The whole lemon/olive oil drink described in the last chapter has helped many persons with CFIDS, HIV, candidiasis, cancer and other conditions. Several factors emerge in all these conditions.

1. Toxic colon - too alkaline - no bifidus, B longum and other bifido-bacteria. This results in low butyrate and acetic acid levels.

2. No acidophilus can be found in stool samples. This means the liver is toxic and is dumping toxins in the bile in the small intestines. These toxins in the bile kill off the acidophilus as fast as you can swallow the probiotics.

3. Body temperature runs low, below 98.6°F. The lower the body temperature, the less responsive is the immune system. Chronic low body temperature is often an indication of a toxic colon and liver. Whole lemon/olive oil drink (to detoxify the liver), Cayenne (red pepper), Venus Fly Trap extract, cold showers and exercise all help to increase and normalize body temperature. Cayenne, Venus fly-trap extract and cold showers all stimulate the body to produce Interleukin 1 (IL-1), the main switch of the immune system that turns up the thermostat and increases body heat.

4. **Selenium**: Natural plant based selenium found in whole foods or whole food supplements can be very beneficial by improving immune function and increasing the conversion of Thyroid hormone T4 to T3. **Researchers have found that selenium improves the function of neutrophils, a type of white blood cells that controls candida albicans and other kinds of yeast infections**. Food sources; Brazil nuts contain about 100 mcg per nut. Other Seafood is a good source of selenium also. Food based supplements: **Phytosel** (from hydroponicly grown Indian Mustard Greens by Nucycle) or SelenoMax or similar yeast derived selenium. A good choice is to eat 4 **Brazil Nuts** daily that will provide about 400 mcg of 100% natural selenium. Phytosel is distributed to health care professionals and health food stores by Ojibwa Tea of Life Denver CO (303-322-7930)

For adults 400 mcg of 100% plant derived natural selenium daily is sufficient for preventing selenium deficiency and 800 to 1200 mcg daily is for therapeutic use. The only selenium products I found effective are plant based - high-selenium mustard greens or high selenium yeast. At 800 to 1000 mcg daily, the organic plant based selenium products usually resolve yeast infections in a few weeks.

5. In a condition called candidiasis, there is an overproduction of Interleukin 6 and often too many antibodies. There is a slow response from the macrophages and neutrophils, two types of white blood cells that control yeast infections. Several persons

51

have had benefit from Beta **1,3 glucan**, a substance derived from the membranes of the common baker's yeast, not to be confused with candida albicans. **Beta glucan activates macrophage function**. An effective dose is 100 to 200 mg or more daily. **IP6**, like selenium, also **improves Neutrophil function** and helps to control yeast and other types of infections and, like garlic, increases Natural Killer cell function. To reduce IL-6 levels, consider **rice bran or raw wheat germ**. Be sure it is fresh, sealed in a package, vacuum or nitrogen packed. Place in freezer or refrigerate after opening. **Cayenne also reduces IL-6 levels.**

6. Therapeutic foods are **raw garlic cloves**. Use one clove 3 times a day. Slice it on rye crisp and eat with marinated artichokes. Also baked onions, French onion soup and asparagus are all very helpful. Enemas with garlic and vinegar added daily. The cure for chronic candidiasis can be found in focusing on three areas - work to obtain floating stools, yellow urine and a normal body temperature. As the body temperature returns to normal, macrophage and Neutrophil function will improve and the chronic candidiasis will go away.

7. Liquid Ionic Minerals - 1 tsp. twice daily (from the Dead Sea from SGS Research or Marine Minerals - 15 drops twice daily.

Prescription drugs are also available to kill fungal infection. Over the counter supplements include caprylic acid from coconut oil, Oregamax, Oil of oregano, LDM-100 (Lomatium dissectum) and thyme to kill candida in the head. Remember that for immune reconstitution to prevent reoccurring flare-ups of yeast infections to use both IP6 and plant-derived selenium to improve Neutrophil and macrophage function. Immune reconstitution is a better alternative than giving up all carbohydrates, a choice that can lead to chronic depression.

Colitis

Colitis can be caused by viruses like Cytomegalovirus (CMV), other infections or toxic bile or food allergies. Have yourself tested for leaky gut syndrome and food allergies. Use vegetable digestive enzymes with meals, use Vitamin A - 2 tablespoons of plain (not emulsified) cod liver oil daily and butyrate capsules (Ecological Formulas or Nutricology). Vitamin D – 5000 i.u. to 10,000 i.u daily. Use 3 capsules of Butyrate with each meal. Take acidophilus supplements with each meal and follow the diet to increase acidophilus and bifido-bacteria in the intestines. Cultured cabbage juice. Use 1/2 cup 2 or 3 times daily. Consider supplements listed for Leaky Gut Syndrome.

Constipation

Occasional and mild conditions: **high fiber diet** and drink more water. **Exercise** and **water** will reduce inflammation and help move food through the G.I. tract.

Chronic and severe conditions: Check for food allergies. **Avoid food you are allergic to and all refined carbohydrates.** Reduce your dependency on drugs that reduce intestinal mucin production. Use Bioplasma homeopathic cell salts. **Bioplasma** (Hyland's) contains all 12 of Dr. Schuessler's essential cell salts - use 20 tablets under the tongue 3 times daily. This will increase moisture in the stools.

Other treatments: Aloe Vera juice - 1/2 cup before bedtime. Castor oil - 1 tsp. before bedtime or 6 capsules. **A glass of high-fiber prune juice after meals.** Diet - emphasize squash, carrots and pumpkin and foods high in FOS, calcium and fiber that support bifido bacteria growth in the colon. This will increase production of intestinal mucus.

Common and lesser known causes of constipation - mega dosing on Vitamin C. I know 4 people with were long time users (over 3 years) of 5 to 10 grams of Vitamin C daily and were chronically constipated for over 2 years. When they reduced the dose of Vitamin C to 500 mg daily or less, they were no longer constipated. Certain drugs like aspirin, if used every day and to excess, can reduce intestinal mucus production and contribute to constipation and intestinal inflammation. **For a natural source of Vitamin C that includes dozens of co-factors, use Amla, Rosehips, Acerola cherries, or oranges.**

A lack of production of intestinal mucus is a major cause of constipation. **A lack of ionized calcium and magnesium is another cause of chronic constipation**. You need foods high in FOS to increase calcium and magnesium absorption. These foods are **onions, garlic, artichokes and asparagus.** For the cure, use these along with foods that are naturally high in calcium and fiber. Use plain cod liver oil daily. Cod liver oil is far preferable to taking vitamin A and D capsules. In addition to vitamin A and D, Cod liver oil has an ample supply of DHA/EPA that supports circulation and immune function.

When all else fails as a treatment for constipation, try mixing a fiber formula (psyllium etc) with high fiber prune juice and drink this 1 to 3 times a day before meals. Eat lots of steamed or boiled vegetables and avoid protein powders, grains, bread, and pasta until bowel movements return to normal. I have seen good results with **Colon Comfort Formula**, a probiotic, flaxseed and inulin based formula (Ojibwa Tea of Life, Denver CO).

Crohns disease

Crohns disease is a chronic inflammation of a section of the intestines. Two persons told me they cured themselves of Crohns disease by drinking 1/3 cup of coconut milk 3 times daily. Another person cured himself by giving up all grains, but especially avoiding all grains with gluten (wheat, oats and barley). Emphasis on baked or boiled squash, pumpkin, and carrots. Cultured cabbage juice. Use 1/2 cup 2 or 3 times daily. Supplements: Butyrate 3 capsules 3 times daily (Ecological Formulas or Nutricology), Take probiotics with meals. Vitamin D 5000 to 10,000 i.u. daily.

Diarrhea - chronic

There are three common causes of diarrhea. One is infection of the small and large intestines. The second is metabolic. For infections, see "Infections - Intestinal" below. For metabolic, a calcium deficiency is a major cause. Eat foods high in calcium, Tofu, plain yogurt, canned salmon and sardines -with the bones in it. Use Coral calcium powder, one-half teaspoon in a glass of water once or twice daily. The third cause of diarrhea is food allergies when your immune system rebels against certain foods and literally tries to wash it out of the body. Have yourself tested for food allergies and avoid these foods.

Treatments - temporary - use charcoal capsules - 3 with a glass of water 3 to 5 times daily. Use the charcoal capsules along with a simple diet of black tea, no sugar added and whole grain bread toasted well - with no butter added for one to 3 days until the diarrhea has stopped. You may add Stevia to the tea for a sweetener. Also very helpful is pure citrus pectin (no sugar added)

- use one tsp. in a glass of water 3 to 5 times daily. Avoid all sugar and fruits, except for lemons and limes. Add plain yogurt to your diet when the diarrhea has stopped and gradually add items from the diet plan in this book one at a time. Avoid the ones that cause problems.

SB Normal Stool Formula - A rain forest tree sap stops diarrhea

An extract from a tree in the rain forest of South America has been used by local natives for decades to treat diarrhea or watery stools from multiple causes, including Cholera, according to Dr. Thomas Carlson MD, MS. The sap, blood red in color, is derived from the tree, Croton lechleri, and has been used in Iquitos, Peru, for different types of diarrhea.

For diarrhea related to an infectious agent known as Clostridium Difficile, use the probiotic Saccharmyces Boulardii. – It is found in health food stores. (Jarrow Formulas offers this probiotic) For metabolic diarrhea, a diet of cooked rice and natural applesauce will sometimes resolve the condition.

Digestive aids - natural

Red beets are a source of betaine hydrochloride to help with protein digestion (i.e consider red beet powder or crystals sprinkled over meals). Ginger root is a source of protein digestive enzymes. Raw pineapple is a source of bromelain for protein digestion. Cayenne stimulates the whole digestive process. Lemon juice - helps ionize minerals in foods for assimilation and increases saliva for the digestion of carbohydrates. Apple cider and other forms of vinegar also help in the assimilation of minerals. Gentian root - herbal bitters - helps liver function and digestion. Any of these alone or in combination may be used with meals. Blackstrap molasses is also a source of betaine hydrochloride. A teaspoon of blackstrap molasses in a cup of hot water is an excellent digestive aid. Fennel seed may be added. You can also use vegetarian digestive enzymes or pancreatin tablets. **Avoid Papain (from Papaya seeds) if your stomach is sensitive.**

Gall Stones

Lemon juice will dissolve gallstones. Use 1/4 cup once or twice daily. Dilute with as little water as possible and take on an empty stomach. Take a couple tablespoon of olive oil before bedtime.

Have your physician recheck for gallstones after 7 days. Follow with whole lemon/olive oil drink if needed.

Gas - intestinal - upper

Infections and fermentation in the stomach or wrong food combinations are a common causes of upper intestinal gas. Combine proteins with vegetables or whole grains with vegetables. Avoid combining sugar or fruit with vegetables. Eat fruit or sweets alone one hour before meals or 2 hours after. Try eating one or tow food at a meal and avoid Smorgasbords.

Treatments - temporary - charcoal capsules - 3 or more with a small amount of water. One tablespoon of apple cider vinegar or the juice of half of lemon with a small amount of water. Digestive enzymes - vegetarian derived enzymes - take 3 to 5 tablets or capsules. Fennel and/or wild yam extract - 20 to 40 drops. Ginger root - 1 tablespoon of fresh grated root eaten or made into a tea. Note: if your urine is clear, (not yellow), it indicates a lack of bifido-bacteria in the colon and a deficiency of B vitamins that are needed to support hydrochloric acid production.

When all else fails, take 10 drops of grapefruit extract in 4 ounces of water. Take this 4 times a day for 3 days or longer if needed. Grapefruit seed extract will kill off most infections in the stomach and small intestines. Check your body temperature to see if it is normal.

Infections - intestinal

An abundance of friendly flora in both the small and large intestines is essential for long-term prevention or control of intestinal infections. Many infections including parasites can be directly treated with antibiotics and prescription drugs while others like HHV-6, CMV, hepatitis, EBV and others are more difficult to eliminate. Vitamin D – take 5000 to 10,000 i.u. daily to restore immune function.

For parasites:

1.) Raw garlic - 3 cloves daily with rye crisp or other whole grain crackers. 2.) Myrrh – 20 drops in water 3 times a day – kills parasites and worms. 3.) Castor oil capsules - place in a freezer and take 3 capsules once a day before bedtime. 4.) Wormwood - artemesia annua - 30 drops of extract in water 3 times daily. 5.)

Avoid sweets, parasites love sugar. 6.) Consider having a Colonic done by a professional colon therapist.

Viral infections:

1. **Grapefruit seed extract** is highly effective. Use 10 drops in 4 ounces of water 3 times a day spaced exactly 8 hours apart for 5 to 7 days. Because it depresses saliva pH, grapefruit seed extract should not be used continuously.

2. **Apple cider vinegar or sauerkraut juice or the juice of a whole lemon** - use one or two tablespoons of apple cider vinegar in 4 ounces of water or the juice of a whole lemon 3 times daily *exactly 8 hours apart or drink 4 ounces of sauerkraut juice 8 hours apart.* Bee propolis capsules can be also used 2 or 3 times daily. Bee propolis is what the bees use in their hives as a natural disinfectant. *Keeping the timing of these doses consistent and 8 hours apart is critical for success.*

3. **Chlorophyll** - kills many kinds of viral and other infections. Use one or two tablespoons in 4 ounces of water three times a day.

4. **Cryptosporidium** diarrhea- consider Colostrum Specific (Jarrow Formulas). Take 3 capsules 3 times a day 8 hours apart for 3 weeks. Use only on an empty stomach. Drink Black tea and burned toast until stools are solid. Add no sugar or butter. Then follow diet plan in this book - avoid sugar for 3 weeks.

Note: Avoid cutting raw chicken and other meats then using the same knife to make a salad. This is an easy way to spread salmonella and other infections. See your doctor for other options.

Insomnia - a gut issue?

1. **Sun tanning (very important)** - naturally outdoors or in a sun tanning salon (UVA). If indoor sun tanning is used, try to obtain 20 minutes twice a week. Sun tanning increases vitamin D and improves the utilization of calcium, calms the nerves and helps normalize body temperature. Vitamin D – consider taking 5000 to 10,000 i.u. daily

2. **Exercise (aerobic)** - talk a long walk or bicycle ride for about 20 to 30 minutes before retiring to bed. Note: weight lifting won't work and will temporarily increase cortisone levels.

3. **Coral Calcium or Calcium Lactate - Other forms of calcium may not work!** Coral Calcium – take 2 or 3 capsules or ½

tsp in the evening. Cottage cheese is a good source of natural calcium lactate (1/2 cup as a late evening snack).

4. **Cherry Juice** – drink 6 ounces before bedtime – contains natural melatonin, a hormone that induces sleep.

Other very helpful treatments for Insomnia

1. Essential oils – Lavender and/or Marjoram. Place a few drops on your nostrils or the pillow or use a diffuser.

2. Elderberry extract - 2 or 3 tablespoons in the evening or drink elderberry tea.

3. Magnetic pads - Place pad on back or stomach area for about one hour in the evening with the north pole (negative) energy facing the body. Magnetic pads designed by Dr. Wm. Philpott MD are available from Envirotech - 405-390-3499.

4. Melatonin - 1 to 3 mg before bedtime. Start with the lowest dose and work up. Timed released is preferred.

5. Herbal teas: one teaspoon of Scullcap or hops in hot water. Steep for 10 minutes. Strain and drink.

Scullcap would be my first choice. Do not use sedative herbs with coffee, tea, any product containing caffeine, ma huang, gotu kola or other herbal stimulants or diet pills (to lose weight).

Consider sun tanning, exercise, cherry juice, and coral calcium or calcium lactate (cottage cheese/plain yogurt) as first choices. Avoid sugar/sweets before bedtime. See my book **"Insomnia, fatigue and Cell Phone Towers."** for information on how microwave radiation is waking up millions of people every night and how to stop it from affecting you.

Kidney stones

Use whole lemon/olive oil drink and 500 mg of magnesium oxide twice daily. Herb: Chanca Piedra – 500 mg 3X

Leaky Gut Syndrome

Specifics: Diet high in foods that contain fiber, FOS, calcium and carotenoids, not just beta-carotene. Gelatin, Cod liver oil, raw cabbage, sauerkraut juice or cultured cabbage juice or raw potato juice, L-glutamine with biotin, Horsetail herb - 2 capsules 2 or 3 times daily - also helps with skin, hair and nails. Sun tanning - outdoors or indoors in a tanning salon - use the slower tanning equipment - 15 minutes twice a week. Other: Slippery elm tea, Ojibwa tea or Essiac, Witch hazel tea and/or aloe vera juice. Vitamin D – consider taking 5000 to 10,000 i.u. daily

Osteoporosis - a gut issue?

Osteoporosis affects 25 million Americans and is caused by a deficiency of calcium and other minerals, yet taking large quantities of calcium and even estrogen does not always solve the problem. Have you ever wondered why people with osteoporosis also have food allergies or are intolerant to certain foods?

Major causes of osteoporosis are a toxic colon (too alkaline - low butyrate levels), lack of bifido-bacteria that is critical for mineral absorption, leaky gut syndrome and malabsorption. Malabsorption is an inability of the gastrointestinal tract to absorb adequate amounts of calcium, magnesium and other important minerals needed for healthy bones. FOS, Sun tanning, Cod Liver oil and Coral calcium powder should be used daily. Scientific studies have clearly established that FOS increases calcium and magnesium absorption. This is because FOS supports bifidus and bifido-bacteria that produce a wide range of acids that assist in mineral absorption. Are your stools floating yet and is your urine yellow (without taking B vitamins)? If not, you have a mineral malabsorption condition caused by a lack of bifido-bacteria (Bifidus, B longum etc) in the colon.

A midwife who helps deliver babies told me that she can always tell when women take over the counter calcium supplements. She finds calcium deposits in the placenta. When the women eat yogurt and get their calcium from foods and natural sources, this does not happen. This is the problem with many fractionalized supplements. Calcium never appears alone in nature. It always comes with other minerals in whole food sources. The same problem exists with many man-made vitamins. Chemists synthesize large quantities of vitamins without including naturally occurring co-factors. When it comes to vitamins, more is not better, less is better when it is derived from whole food sources and is balanced.

Stovetop Oat Bran will do more for your health than a product like "Total" that is packed with synthetic vitamins. We must return to whole food supplements to better maintain balance and homeostasis of the gastrointestinal tract.

Buy super foods and whole food supplements only that contain naturally occurring vitamins and minerals. (i.e Cod liver oil, brewers yeast, rose hips or amla, wheat germ, coral calcium, spirulina, chlorella etc) – you got the idea. Trust supplements made by nature and not by slick marketers who like to borrow someone else's research to promote their products. Make them prove by research that their products do what they claim they can do. Vitamin D – consider taking 5000 to 10,000 i.u. daily

Parasites - see "Infections - intestinal

Saliva pH - acid

Use whole lemon olive oil drink in the morning. Eat foods naturally high in calcium and take Coral calcium in the evening. If saliva pH does not come back to normal in 7 days, try Lime water (calcium hydroxide) - use 1 teaspoon in a large glass of water once or twice daily until saliva pH is normal at 6.4 to 6.8 as measured between meals. pH tape (5.5 to 8.5) Micro Essential Labs, NY. Resources for limewater: For health food stores contact Baar Limewater 610-873-4591 or Nutritional Counselors of America, PO Box 155, Spencer, TN 38585

Ulcers -

One half cup of cultured cabbage juice 3 times a day or the juice of raw potatoes - same quantity. Eat foods that increase production of intestinal mucus, a protective film that prevents and helps treat ulcers - foods high in calcium and carotenoids (orange and dark green veggies), FOS and fiber. Avoid fried foods and salt. The application of the North Pole side of a permanent magnet (3000 to 4000 gauss) to the area that is sore will reduce inflammation and help in healing. If you have H. pylori, drink 1/3 cup coconut milk 3 times daily or see your physician for a treatment. Lauric acid in coconut oil or milk kills H pylori.

A concluding thought – eat only when you are hungry, eat slowly and chew your food well, eat wholesome organic foods that are not genetically modified or sprayed with pesticides and herbicides, do not mix too many different foods together at the same time. Thank God daily

References:

1. James Balch MD "Prescription for Nutritional Healing" P. 340 (Avery Publishing Group, Garden City Park, NY)
2. Stedman's Medical Dictionary (Webster's New World, NY)
3. Eseverri JL et al; Allergol Immunopathol 1999 Mar-Apr;27(2):104-11 (Barcelona, Spain)
4. Bachert C; Clin Exp Allergy 1998 Dec;28 Suppl 6:15-19
5. Ohkuba K et al; Rhinology 1998 Dec;36(4):156-61
6. Takamatu S et al; Inflamm Res 1998 May;47(5):221-6
7. Bischoff SC et al; Dig Dis Sci 1997 Feb;42(2):394-403
8. National Library of Medicine
9. Barcelo A et al; Gut 2000 Feb;46(2):218-224
10. Venkatraman A et al; Scand J Gastroenterol 1999 Nov;34(11):1087-92
11. Kirlan WG et al; J Nutr 1999 Oct;129(10):1827-35
12. Compher CW et al; JPEN J Parenter Enteral Nutr 1999 Sep-Oct;23(5):269-77
13. Acidophilus and Colon Health, David Webster; Hygeia Publishing, 800-943-0054.
14. Naaeder SB et al, West Afr J Med 1998 Jul-Sep;17(3):165-7
15. The Garden Within, by Keith Sehnert MD. (Health World Magazine, Burlingame, CA)
16. Health Benefits of FOS, by Robert Crayhon; Keats Publishing, New Canaan, CT.
17. Fallingborg J et al; J Pediatr Gastroenterol Nutr 1990 Aug;11(2):211-4
18. Bech K et al; "The pH and acidity of feces in colorectal neoplasms," Ugeskr Laeger 1990 Jan 15;152(3):161-2
19. Konlee M; Progressive Health News, 1999 (Oct 1st) Vol 2, No 10.
20. Pisai Egyetem et al; Orv Hetil, 1990 Sep 9;131(36):1959-64.
21. Bovee-Oudenhoven IM et al; J Nutr 1999 Mar:129(3):607-12
22. Rani B et al; Nutr Health 1998;12(2):97-105
23. "Biotherapeutic effects of probiotic bacteria on candidiasis in immunodeficient mice," by Wagner Rd et al; Infect Immun 1997 Oct;65(10):4165-72
24. "Dietary Calcium Phosphate Stimulates Intestinal Lactobacilli..." Bovee-Oudenhoven et al; J Nutr 1999 Mar;129(3):607-12
25. IP6 - Nature's Revolutionary Cancer Fighter, by A.M. Shamsiddin MD (Kensington Books)
26. Eggleton P; Anticancer Res 1999 Sep-Oct;19(5A):3711-5
27. Matsura Y; J Nutr Sci Vitamiinol (Toyko) 1998 Jun:44(3):423
28. Venter CS et al; J Nutr 1990 Sep;120(9):1046-53
29. ImmunoPro, 2161 Dryden Rd, El Cajon, CA 92020

Other books by Conrad LeBeau

Immune Restoration Handbook – 3rd edition

By Conrad LeBeau and Dr. Ronald Peters MD. A how to do it book - based on 20 years of research. 26 chapters. Covers the immune system in detail – how it works. Immune based, herbal and nutritional therapies for candidiasis, hepatitis, cancer, hiv, adrenal and thyroid dysfunction, restoring intestinal health, pH balancing, liver and colon cleansing, food allergies, common household items to fight infections and much more. Plant based selenium, the candida cure, fresh flax oil, aloe vera and honey for preventing and treating cancer. Covers bio-oxidative therapies. How to increase glutathione levels - the body's main antioxidant. 268 pages. 8.5" X 11". $24.95

Hydrogen Peroxide and Aloe Vera plus Other Home Remedies.

Prevent and treat over 50 health conditions with bio-oxidative therapies (hydrogen peroxide and ozone) and other remedies including aloe vera, honey, molasses, grapefruit seeds, coral calcium, limewater, milk of magnesia, birch water, flaxseed oil, brazil nuts, garlic, oregano, cayenne, wakame and lemons 64 pages. $7.95

Insomnia, fatigue and Cell Phone Towers

Microwave radiation from cell phone towers can cause health-related problems including - insomnia, shallow sleep, fatigue, adrenal exhaustion, loss of mental focus, oxidative stress, depressed immunity, reduced testosterone levels, endocrine dysfunction, elevated stress hormones (cortisol), headaches, impaired vision, hypertension, asthma and heart disease. Case reports and interviews. How to keep microwave radiation out of your home is discussed. 48 pages $4.95 ea

Natural Remedies for Intestinal Health
64 pages - you are reading it $6.95 ea

To Order with a credit card – 414-231-9817

Conrad LeBeau,
10240 W National Ave #1896
West Allis WI 53227

Add $3 for media mail or $5 for priority mail per order.
Author's affiliated websites – lebeaubooks.com
keephopealive.org